# BEING the SHOPPER

# BEING the SHOPPER

## Understanding the Buyer's Choice

# Phil Lempert

JOHN WILEY & SONS, INC.

Published by John Wiley & Sons, Inc., New York.
Published simultaneously in Canada.

ISBN 0-471-15135-1

Printed in the United States of America.

10  9  8  7  6  5  4  3  2  1

To

My father, Sol,
*for teaching me to aim my dreams high*

My mother, Lillian,
*for believing in my dreams and nurturing them*
and

My wife, Laura,
*for helping me realize my dreams.*

# PREFACE

I have no doubt that I have the best job in the world. I get to walk up and down the aisles of supermarkets, introduce myself to shoppers like you or me, and listen to what they like and don't like about the foods they eat and the stores they shop in. I am introduced on television and at events worldwide as "the supermarket guru." There is no formal training for becoming a supermarket guru. It was a title given to me, one of the first times I appeared on a network news program, because of my specialization: understanding packaged goods, the storefront, and the consumer. My career in the food world spans some twenty-five years as purveyor, salesman, marketer, consultant, and journalist.

*Being the Shopper* is a book about the importance of the consumer, based on the idea that the time has come to refocus marketing and advertising on the people they affect and on the way we shop. The pages of this book are filled with insights gleaned from shoppers, consumer panel surveys, and industry experts, as well as with what I've learned about the basics of human nature. It is a book about marketing, advertising, and consumer behavior that will bring marketers and brand managers closer to your consumers. As consumers yourselves, you will learn much about what motivates you to buy.

This book is necessary reading for all marketers today, given the failure rate for new product introductions; new retail formats, the Internet as a resource for information and acquiring, and the inefficiencies of advertising have reached staggering and wasteful proportions. As I'll show, success is not about following the money—it's about following the shopper.

# CONTENTS

# INTRODUCTION

# Why "Being the Shopper" Is So Important

In this book, I look at the supermarket as a laboratory for shaping a stellar brand, and I show you how to think and act like the real consumers who make split-second decisions between your brand and that of the competition. This book teaches you how to interact with shoppers effectively and to learn from their feedback, shaping your brand and your message to resonate with them. Ultimately, the goal is to be the shopper, seeing your brand from their perspective in order to learn exactly what they want—and how to deliver it.

In *Being the Shopper,* composite consumers, based on real members of my SupermarketGuru.com consumer panel, will take you—the brand managers, retailers, and marketers of the world—

on an enlightening trip inside their minds and help you explore the buying habits of a diverse array of shoppers. The plan is to challenge your traditional methods of understanding consumer behavior by making you feel what it's like to *be* the actual shopper. You will develop a new approach to understanding consumer behavior to increase the likelihood that the shopper will buy your products.

Right now, the trend in marketing is analysis—looking at focus-group data, spending endless hours crunching numbers that can be six months old. The truth is that listening to consumers themselves is an overlooked, invaluable tool. It's never been more necessary than it is right now: The number of new products introduced each year has increased at a breakneck speed. For example, in 1990, there were 15,879 new products introduced into supermarkets, but, by 2000, the number of new products had jumped to 31,431 (Marketing Resource, Naples, New York). With a new product introduction failure rate of 80 percent, it's clear that analysis alone is not the key to marketing success. You need to get out from behind your computer and get into a store to see what is going on with *real* shoppers.

*The reality that marketers must accept is that this is a shopper-driven world, but we're ignoring the real shopper. Too many brand people spend too much time explaining why certain economics and trends occurred. This process serves as a one-way mirror into the past, and locks brands into the never-never land of being stuck in process.*

Although focus groups can be a valuable tool for idea generation, too often they are used to simply validate or justify brand marketers' ideas. Many of our professional marketing and advertising educations have trained us not to think as a shopper would but rather, to think inside the box. Thinking *inside the box* is a time-consuming process that allows marketers to justify their own existence, and to position products and trend events. Too many

---

### YOU ARE STUCK IN PROCESS WHEN:

- Deadlines make you cringe.
- You enjoy reading about products in *Consumer Reports* more than you enjoy buying them.
- You enjoy discussing a problem more than you enjoy solving it.

---

marketers spend too much of their time presenting consumer data based on past purchasing behavior or explaining why a new product or ad campaign didn't work. While these are uncomfortable discussions, they are still safe ones—the problem is that they're about the past. Many marketers avoid what I call *consumer evolution*—investigating what effect the current and future trends might have on a particular brand or business.

Great marketers possess the skill of listening, as well as the ability to approach consumers. You must be able to walk up to a shopper and ask, "Why did you buy this?" You'll find that hearing the

---

### IT'S ABOUT LISTENING!

If you studied marketing or advertising in college or graduate school, you sat through a couple of courses in consumer behavior that mostly focused on understanding the types of question and math used to extrapolate any findings that a consumer survey wanted to achieve from just about any data. You most likely did not learn how to talk with real consumers, and you did not learn how to listen. To find out what shoppers are *really* thinking, you must learn the art of listening. The word *listening* implies a *passive* act of taking in the content of a person's communication. The reality is that good listening is a very *active* process of responding to total messages—it includes listening with your ears to words and observing with your eyes to interpret body language.

---

answer can be exciting, rewarding, and invigorating, and that the most valuable answers are those that are unexpected. Your goal as marketer is to learn to listen well, without taking personal offense of complaints; the reasons for negative reactions will be the most valuable things you can learn from shoppers.

Even when marketers do approach the shopper, they often only present their own positions, failing to take in the shoppers' reactions or needs. As you learn to *be* the shopper, you'll find that communication must be a two-way medium. There are three steps to successfully communicating with the shopper. First, know what you want to achieve—that is, what kind of shopper reaction do you want: information, awareness? Second, find out what the shopper wants to get from your message. Third, discover how you can both get what you want.

 As you learn to listen and to approach, you'll get closer and closer to being the shopper. Being the shopper is about synthesizing the ability to approach real shoppers with the act of listening to even the most negative reactions. Ultimately, the goal is to put yourself in the hearts, minds, and souls of the consumers who are wandering the aisles and waiting in the checkout lines.

## Understanding Shopping Behavior

Part of listening to a shopper involves understanding their biases, because shopping (and buying) patterns are a result of the consumer's learning and communication experiences. Before a shopper enters a store, he or she has stored a lifetime of marketing messages that will influence buying decisions. These messages range from advertising that has raised the shopper's awareness of product features, to information that he or she has learned from the Internet, to a corporate philosophy that he or she respects. A friend's recommendation might secure the shopper's purchase of a particular brand.

## The Three Categories of "Selling" Language

In addition to these biases, there are three main factors that affect the shopper once he or she enters the store. These three factors comprise a selling language that marketers must coordinate and control in order to influence the shopper. These three variables are: visual, auditory, and kinesthetic. The *visual* message is the easiest and most commonly used tool for attracting a consumer. Seeing a picture of what's inside the box reduces the anxiety of purchase, and enables shoppers to see what you are selling. For example, a vivid photo of a mouth-watering dish of grilled salmon with a dill sauce on a frozen-food package is a proven method for attracting shoppers who want to buy a frozen salmon dinner. The *auditory* component is the familiar music and voice that are integrated into the television and radio commercials. This component signals to the shopper that the product is designed just for him or her. If you want to sell to a baby boomer, use the Rolling Stones. If you're selling to a baby boomer's parent, Frank Sinatra would be much more effective.

Communicating through visuals and auditory methods is Marketing 101, and most marketers understand how to use these methods, but the most powerful and underutilized brand messaging is the third category—*kinesthetics*. Communicating kinesthetically induces shoppers to *feel* your message. It's the energy that can build a relationship because of interactive motion. A good way to think about using this approach is to use the analogy of starting a brand relationship the same way strangers who meet for the first time might warmly shake hands.

 **Ask yourself, when was the last time was that you intentionally stopped buying a product that you liked? Remember, shoppers want to feel good about the products they buy and the benefits these products deliver. Understanding that shoppers' emotional needs are as critical as their practical needs is essential if you want to make those shoppers your customers. Relate to them.**

A great example of marketing that integrated listening to the shopper *and* responding with persuasive selling language is the case of olive oil. In the mid-1980s, olive oil was just beginning its meteoric rise. Researchers speculated that olive oil had heart-protective properties and that, by replacing oils high in saturated fats with olive oil, blood cholesterol levels would drop and the amount of HDL-cholesterol (which helps prevent coronary heart disease) would actually increase. This was terrific news for a product category that was struggling, and the timing was perfect, as consumers were fleeing to nonfat and low-cholesterol everything. The question facing olive-oil marketers was how to communicate these benefits.

### MARKETING OLIVE OIL THAT'S LIGHT ON THE OLIVES

Importers of olive oil have been handed a tricky marketing challenge. They've got a hot product in the no-cholesterol derby—a key ingredient in one of the most vaunted European cuisines, a product venerated since at least the Golden Age of Greece—yet Americans complain that olive oil tastes too much like, well, olives.

But wait. The people at Filippo Berio, the No. 2 brand in the country, may have an answer. What if they held in-store demonstrations with a dessert that uses olive oil instead of butter? An American dessert. A classic American dessert. A pound cake. "We're getting our product into the consumer's mouth first," said Phil Lempert, in charge of advertising and promoting the Filippo Berio brand, while Bertolli has relied heavily on television commercials.

The mangia strategy fits with the company's overall marketing plan. As Eugenio Fontana, the patriarch of the Italian family that owned Berio through the Salov North America Corporation, told Lempert, Americans have to "taste it, taste it, taste it." In print ads, Mr. Fontana offers readers free samples of his oil.

Mr. Fontana has probably not had the chance to taste the pound cake, but customers at the Shop Rite of Lincoln Park, New Jersey, had their chance two weeks ago.

*(Continued)*

"One or two customers could not believe that it was made with olive oil," said Larri S. Wolfson, owner of the store. "They expected an off taste and it wasn't there."

Berio will hold some 2,000 in-store demonstrations between now and the end of June at supermarkets along the East Coast, where the company has established its market. The supermarkets, all with in-house bakeries, make the pound cakes from a recipe provided by Berio. Some of the stores find that if they bake extra cakes (labeled "Made with Filippo Berio") consumers will buy them after tasting the square-inch sample.

This sort of faith in the educated consumer is evidenced throughout the campaign, most obviously in the persona of its chief strategist—Phil Lempert.

Mr. Lempert holds a unique position in the advertising world. Making a specialty of food and grocery products (he has about 14 clients and predicts that he will have about $23 million in billings this year), he is also a supermarket analyst who publishes a consumer-trends newsletter, *The Lempert Report*.

Mr. Lempert believes that if the shortest distance between two points is a straight line, than traditional television advertising is a detour. That's not to say he avoids television. He often appears on talk shows, including a recent guest shot on the "Home" show, and even on network and local news. He's there to comment on food issues.

Mr. Lempert's hybrid role—to clients he's an adman; to viewers he's a consumer analyst—may be the perfect way to sell a food product validated by science and romanced by food writers. His print campaign for Berio exploits the European courtliness of Mr. Fontana, as he urges readers to try half-ounce samples of the company's Mild & Light and Extra Virgin olive oil. Instead of the usual clip-out coupon, the ad uses a glued-on picture postcard of Lucca, Italy, with space on the back for the reader's name and address. Mr. Lempert says 135,000 postcards have been mailed so far and that he still receives 5,000 to 9,000 each week.

*Source:* Damon Wright, *New York Times*, April 16, 1989. Copyright © 1989 by the New York Times Co. Reprinted by permission.

As the case history of olive oil illustrates, marketing success is directly affected by shopping and purchasing behavior. This concept may seem obvious, but it's too often ignored because too many marketers are fixated on numbers and focus-group data. In order to be a master marketer today, your focus must be on listening to the shopper—distilling the nuances that enable shoppers to want to build a relationship with your brand and product. Whether it be a package, television commercial, Web site, or taste, the marketing mantra is the same: Connect with a shopper's basic instinct and senses—and they will buy.

Understanding your individual customers intimately is the ultimate goal.

A number of brands ran to market with clinical studies under their arms, shouting out the health benefits along the way. Advertising in health-related magazines like *Prevention* increased sales, but only slightly, and to a micromarket. American shoppers were not quite ready to understand health as food marketing. In fact, most Americans said that they were hesitant about using olive oil, because they believed that the oil actually tasted like olives. As this newspaper article explains, I directed the Filippo Berio effort to bring olive oil to American kitchens. It wasn't until both the Bertolli and Filippo Berio brands listened, accepted these shoppers' reality, and started in-store sampling, that the sales of olive oil took off.

# The Consumer Today

*B*eing the Shopper is about increasing your success in selling your products and services by better understanding the way real shoppers think and act. Yesterday's marketing rules dictated that brand plans define a single target market—for example, trying to sell a particular gourmet chocolate dessert to women 18 to 34 years old, with two children, and a household income of over $75,000. As you become increasingly familiar with your shopper, you'll rely less and less on demographic information. However, in the beginning, it's important to understand the major population trends and their implications for your brands and retail environments. Consider the chart on the next page with U.S. census information. You'll notice some fascinating fluctuations as baby boomers age. The 25- to 34-year-old category is predicted to wane considerably. In this section and in the next chapter, I explore the

### Population Projections by Age

The U.S. Census Bureau's statistics on population projections by age is a fascinating look at future population trends. In this section, I review the major trends that will shape the shoppers of tomorrow.

| Age | 1990 (millions) | 2000 (millions) | 2010 (millions) | Change 1990–2010 (%) |
|---|---|---|---|---|
| All Americans | 248,709 | 275,307 | 299,862 | 20.6 |
| <5 | 18,354 | 18,865 | 20,099 | 9.5 |
| 5–19 | 52,967 | 59,586 | 61,014 | 15.2 |
| 20–24 | 19,020 | 18,518 | 21,151 | 11.2 |
| 25–34 | 43,176 | 37,441 | 38,851 | −10 |
| 35–44 | 37,579 | 44,894 | 39,443 | 5 |
| 45–54 | 25,223 | 37,166 | 44,161 | 75.1 |
| 55–64 | 21,148 | 24,001 | 35,429 | 67.5 |
| 65+ | 31,242 | 34,835 | 39,715 | 27.1 |

*Sources:* U.S. Census Bureau and Bureau of Labor Statistics, 2000.

implications of these population trends and explain how to learn about the actual individuals within these categories.

## Are You Prepared to Sell to *These* Shoppers?

In this section, I review some of the biggest changes over the last two decades within particular demographic groups. These trends are significant because they've created new and unique potential markets. Also, the stark contrast between today and yesterday can feed into ripe marketing opportunities. For instance, many of the women who are likely to return to work shortly after giving birth were raised with traditional stay-at-home moms. This new generation of working mothers may be receptive to brands of food that are quick to assemble, but deliver the home-cooked taste and wholesome nutrition that their mothers valued.

Knowing your shoppers' ages is one thing, but appealing to how they really feel is another thing entirely. As a marketer, you'll be far better attuned to your shoppers if you can understand the difference. I empower my audiences, at every one of my speeches, to understand that the first step in being the shopper is to not form opinions of others based on their ages. Each member of the audience is asked to turn to the person next to them and tell them how old they are. After the nervous laughter, I then ask them to turn back to the same person and tell them how old they feel. Six members of the audience (three men and three women) are asked to voluntarily to share the information with the entire group.

In the thousands of times I have presented this exercise, my volunteers have always reinforced my message by proving the difference between how old someone is and how old they feel. On average, these people feel 10 years younger than they actually are.

Appealing to emotions of a consumer will *always* be more effective than developing a marketing campaign based on an age classification.

## Changes in Motherhood

One major trend in recent years has affected women of childbearing age. In 1976, according to the U.S. Census Bureau, 31 percent of mothers returned to the outside-the-home workforce within a year of giving birth. In 1998, the figure had risen to 58.7 percent. For women with a college education, statistics show that 68 percent will return to the workforce before their child celebrates his or her first birthday.

**Look for opportunities to market to these working moms. Some of them belong to the category of women who want it all: the career and the family. Others may be struggling to make ends meet, and face the challenges**

of single parenthood. If they find a superior product that meets their needs, they'll buy it, week after week. You might also try getting to them through their kids—as I discuss in Chapter 2, teens and preteens have increasingly become decision makers within the retail realm.

## Men's Roles as Parents

In addition to trends in motherhood, men's roles in raising children have changed dramatically. Mediamark Research reports that the percentage of male homemakers (defined as the person in the household who does most of the shopping) reached 30.3 percent in 2000, up from 15 percent in 1985. Most of these male homemakers live alone, live with children, or live with other men.

 Learn about the stay-at-home father. Does he act like a big kid himself—indulging the children with junk food and special privileges that mom wouldn't tolerate? Does he, like many stay-at-home moms, keep up with the latest trends in childrearing by reading parenting magazines? Does he grapple with issues of masculinity, or does he reject Rambo and other stereotypes of macho behavior? Who are his role models?

## Single-Person Households

Fifty years ago, single-person households made up just 10 percent of the population. According to the *2000 Census of Population and Housing*, those shoppers now account for over 25 percent of households. Single-person households are increasing most rapidly of all demographic groups; that trend is expected to continue. Women are the majority (58 percent) of those who live alone, and half of those are 65 or over. In contrast, of the men who live alone, almost half (47 percent) are 25 to 44 years old. U.S. Census Bureau projections to the year 2020 show a dramatic increase in the number of middle-aged singles. Single-household women aged 45 to 64 will increase by 65 percent, and single-household men age 45 to 64 will increase by 83 percent.

**Like shifts in parenthood, this trend in living alone is a new phenomenon. How might you appeal to this new and emerging group? Like many working mothers, they likely were raised to value family and community. As I** discuss in Chapter 5, making customers feel like part of a larger community is a powerful marketing tool.

## Getting Married Later

The median age for marriage has increased from age 20.8 for women in 1970, to age 25.1 in 2000. Men's marrying age has increased from 23.2 in 1970 to 26.8 in 2000. Obviously, there are a multitude of reasons that people are waiting longer to marry, but there is little doubt that this trend allows individuals more time to become established in the workforce before they marry.

**The trend toward getting married later means that there are many twenty-somethings immersed in their careers. Like working mothers, they might have little time for traditional activities like cooking, but still retain a** desire to be healthy. For others, their twenties are an extension of the teenage and college years, with few responsibilities and the desire to remain young and vibrant. Learn about these Peter Pans by reading their magazines—*Maxim* and JANE—watching their television shows and movies, and learning to approach them in their venues.

So far, I've outlined several different population trends. However, knowing these trends and applying them to marketing efforts are two entirely different things. Walking up and down the aisles of a supermarket with a working mom, male homemaker, single shopper, and late-marrieds will begin to shift your consumer behavior paradigm as you learn to perceive your product through their eyes, ears, and taste buds. For example, each of these individuals might have one purchase in common with the others—Coca-Cola. How they make the purchase will vary drastically—for instance, the late-married might choose a two-liter bottle of Diet Coke, while the single shopper might choose cans of caffeine-free Coca-Cola. The working mom might choose a single chilled can of Cherry Coke

In your quest to be the shopper, it helps to know what factors draw certain individuals to choose a particular brand over another. Here is a list of what different groups rated as the most important attributes in their food-purchasing decisions:

| Attribute | Groups |
|---|---|
| Nutrition | Women, especially women at home; seniors; nonwhites; shoppers who often cook at home. |
| Price | Household income below $35,000; members of blue-collar households; high-school graduates. |
| Ease of preparation | Cook dinner at home fewer than 4 days/week; frequent microwave users; Southerners. |
| Environmentally responsible packaging | Nonwhites; seniors; women, especially women at home; frequent microwave users; high-school grads. |
| Convenient/easy-to-use packaging | Nonwhites; seniors; high-school grads. |

Source: Grocery Manufacturers of America, Consumers Speak Out, Spring, 1999.

and hide it from her kids because soda is not allowed in her house, while the male homemaker might select Coke in vintage glass bottles, and keep the bottles for his kids' art project.

---

*Knowing these preferences is critical to attracting these shoppers. Use the demographic information and population trends as your starting point for discovering their unique desires and needs. Remember that age and population data are not absolutes, particularly if they contrast dramatically with how the individual shoppers perceive themselves.*

---

PART ONE

# THE SHOPPER

CHAPTER

2

# Selling in a Diverse Economy

In this chapter, I explore several significant age and ethnic groups and how marketers can learn to *be* members of these populations. As I noted in the introduction, age and ethnic demographics alone can be deceiving. But as marketers, you can build on this cursory information to truly understand the shopper.

## Why Kids Are So Important

No question about it, kids have money and they often make brands successful. We want them as consumers. We, as marketers, spend heavily to reach them and try to build a relationship, so why do they seem to be so elusive?

One reason that we often seem to miss the mark in marketing to kids is that, although we put all our money and effort to work to attract them, we do it without *knowing* them. It's far too simple to look up their psychographics, pay someone to hold a couple of focus groups, or even read the latest teen survey. What's harder is actually understanding them, on their terms and in their language.

The impulse of many marketers is to assemble special teen units or teen-marketing task forces. These focus groups are not the same as getting out and observing teens in shopping malls and high schools; watching teen movies and television shows; reading teen magazines; and, most important; reconnecting with your own teen experiences. It's well worth the effort: Parents spend over $300 billion annually on groceries for teenagers alone. In the January 2000 "Report of Teen Research Unlimited Study," *Discount Store News* reported that, in 1999, teens spent $105 billion of their own money and influenced $48 billion in family spending.

---

*If you're wondering why kids are a significant potential market, consider this: Middle income families spend between $9,390 and $9,530 per year on the typical teen.*
**—USDA, "Expenditures on Children by Families"**

---

The first step in learning to be a member of this age group is to know what they buy. Another factor in orienting yourself with teens is learning who they respect and would want to befriend. One of the next steps in learning about today's teens is discovering how they're different and what makes them unique.

---

### ITEMS MOST PURCHASED BY TEENS IN 1999

1. Bubble Gum
2. Clothes
3. Deodorant
4. Fast Food
5. Ice Cream
6. Movie Tickets
7. Shampoo
8. Soft Drinks
9. Toothpaste

---

*Source: tZine Network.*

### WHO'S THE ULTIMATE TEEN BACK-TO-SCHOOL SHOPPING BUDDY IN 2001?

| | |
|---|---|
| Britney Spears | 16% |
| Christina Aguilera | 15 |
| 'NSYNC | 15 |
| Shaquille O'Neil (NBA Star) | 12 |
| Tony Hawk (skateboarder) | 10 |
| The Rock (WWF Star) | 7 |
| Derek Jeter (NY Yankees) | 6 |
| Backstreet Boys | 4 |

*Source: Capital One Back-to-School Spending Pattern Survey,* July 2001.

The obvious technological changes have made them a quicker, savvier, more global generation. Because of their parents' affluence, as well the family's packed schedules, today's teens have been given the power and responsibilities of buying at a far earlier age.

> ***One-third of teenagers own their own computer and 17 percent own their own modem.***
> **—Teenage Research Unlimited, 2000**

The most significant difference—and opportunity—that I have observed with today's teens focuses around their unique and early adaptiveness toward value, savings, and investing. Boomers never had it and, fortunately for their generation, the windfall inheritances and real estate profits will save them. According to a Cornell University study, it is estimated that baby boomers will likely inherit $10 trillion through 2040. GenX, economically forgotten long ago, will have to wait their turn for the benefits of the same windfalls, but this generation got smarter and wealthier faster.

### Average Expenditure of Households (HH)
### with Teens (Ages 14–17) 1997–1998

| Total Household | HH with All Teens | HH with Employed Teens | HH with Nonemployed Teens |
|---|---|---|---|
| Expenditures | $37,860 | $42,450 | $35,220 |
| Food at home | 5,148 | 5,263 | 5,072 |
| Food away from home | 1,741 | 1,995 | 1,620 |
| Clothing | 2,158 | 2,292 | 2,078 |
| Entertainment | 2,347 | 2,844 | 2,078 |

*Source:* Monthly Labor Review, September 2000.

According to the 1997–1998 Consumer Expenditures Survey, 34 percent of teens were employed sometime during the year and had average annual earnings of $2,270. As the chart above shows, households with teens who are employed actually end up spending more per capita than households with nonemployed teens.

Be the Shopper

Because of their technological savvy and their propensity to work, this generation of teenagers will undoubtedly have more savings and economic clout than anyone imagined. But unlike boomers who were easy prey for marketers, or GenXers who had the desire to buy but no money, marketing to teens is tougher and requires a new set of rules—the most important being respect for their knowledge. Marketers have to realize that, although these teens may be the most affluent generation ever, getting those dollars will be the toughest sale your brand has ever pitched.

## Kids, Kids, and More Kids?

In 1990, there was a population peak at 4,158,000 births, coinciding with women of the baby-boom generation moving out of their childbearing years. Birth trends since have continued to decline and will do so until 2007, when estimates call yet again for 4.1 million births, followed by a slight increase to 4.2 million by 2009.

While it is easy to predict that we will always continue to have children, some years four million, some years less, the real information for success will come from understanding where we are culturally. A look at the birth rate in the United States shows a dramatic decline since 1965. The majority of Americans through 1987 were White, with a low birth rate. As we look to the future, a review of the birth rates and population projections across the ethnic mix shows us that marketing to kids (and later, as teens and adults) will be more diverse, harder to execute, and subsequently, more expensive.

The U.S. Census Bureau reports that there are over 27 million 5- to 11-year-olds, and projections for 2005 are that these preteens will be making direct purchases of from $17 billion to over $23 billion. Kids also *directly* influence the purchase of all goods and services to the tune of over $167 billion, with their *indirect* influence thought to be triple that figure. Their expenditures on food and beverages are estimated at about 30 percent of their total spending or close to $5.8 billion per year.

### Projections of the Changing U.S. Ethnic Population

|  | 2000 Population | | 2010 Population | | Growth Increase | |
|---|---|---|---|---|---|---|
|  | Percent | Actual Number (000) | Percent | Actual Number (000) | Percent | Actual Number (000) |
| Asian | 3.9 | 10,620 | 4.8 | 14,436 | 35.9 | 3,816 |
| Hispanic origin | 11.8 | 32,479 | 14.6 | 43,688 | 34.5 | 11,209 |
| American Indian | 0.7 | 2,048 | 0.8 | 2,300 | 12.3 | 252 |
| Black | 12.2 | 33,490 | 12.5 | 37,483 | 11.9 | 3,993 |
| White | 71.4 | 196,670 | 67.3 | 201,956 | 2.7 | 5,286 |

*Note:* Average population growth over this period is 8.9 percent.
*Source:* U.S. Census Bureau.

## GenX Is Interesting, but GenN Is Where the Power Is!

Remember the first time you heard about GenX? As a marketer, your adrenaline pumped and creative juices flowed. You imagined all the cool ideas that were out of the mainstream concepts that you've always wanted to do. And you tried them. And most of them failed.

No question that the rules for marketing to GenX, or any generation for that matter, are different than we imagine. Coupland's book presented a foundation for this generation's emotional and graphic needs. It exposed us to the concept of multitasking before it was defined on our computer screens and accepted by all generations as commonplace.

As I study GenX; there are two marketing rules that I never forget.

### GenX Marketing Rule #1

Boomers are boomers and GenXers are GenXers and never the twain shall meet! GenX does not hate the boomer population, but there is a lot of resentment toward this generation that seems to have it all, with little left for the GenXers.

Those boomers born in 1946 grew up in the 1950s in an environment where Mom stayed at home and divorce was unusual. GenXers defined the latchkey generation and learned how to fend for themselves.

GenX is not about being a slacker, or being distracted and unmotivated. They are the first generation that experienced open family dysfunctionality. They learned to trust no one. They grew up in tight-knit groups where it was truly "one for all, all for one." Brands became the badges not of status, but of belonging.

At the moment, we find ourselves in an unusual sociological predicament. For many generations, the older, more established generation worked hard to provide a better life for the next generation.

In recent generations, it meant a college education versus high school, a house versus an apartment, or a new car versus a used car. It was the generation in power taking care of the next generation. This is not always so with the boomers, who are working hard for themselves to enjoy bigger and better trappings of life.

*(Continued)*

**GenX Marketing Rule #2**

Forget GenX and concentrate on GenN—the networking generation. This is the group that wakes up in the morning not sure if they will be a boomer or an GenXer. They were born between 1961 and 1964, and cross generational lines.

This group has a strong work ethic, grew up with computers and understand how to use them, and is next in line to take over from the burned-out boomers. They are focused, serious about work, and are impatient as they see their boomer bosses wasting away.

They want the boomer jobs and money . . . and will get them, sooner than you think.

As we begin to see the workplace power and money shifting to this generation, expect a tougher and more demanding customer to win, but a harder, less fickle, one to lose.

 **These kids are smart shoppers. As more responsibility has been given to younger latchkey children, not only are they making their own decisions (and sometimes the supermarket brand choices for the whole family), they are gaining confidence in their roles as shoppers. According to the Food Institute Report, February 1998, "Generation Y Goes Shopping," 55 percent of the offspring of baby boomers describe shopping as their favorite activity. These kids, born after 1976, are a generation as large as baby boomers and, in 10 years, will total just over 41 percent of the population.**

Approximately 31 million teens spent $141 billion in 1989. According to the Rand Youth Poll, which has been surveying teen attitudes and behaviors since 1953, spending in this 13- to 19-year-old group should increase steadily through 2005 at a rate of at least 4 percent annually, which will in part be influenced by an increase in the size of the group by three million teens.

## The Never-Aging Baby Boom

*In 1900, life expectancy in the United States was 47.*
*In 2000, it was 77. By 2050, it is projected to be 85.*

The industry we call *marketing and advertising* developed and prospered directly with the birthrate of the boomers, which was a staggering 76 million. Today, the boomers account for 30.2 percent of the American population, and 56.8 percent of household income. Demographers and futurists like Ken Dychtwald, author of *Age Wave*, have long preached the opportunities that can be created by following and satisfying the needs and desires of generations as they mature, evolve, and enter new life stages.

In 1996, the first of the boomers turned 50, creating a momentous birthday celebration for a new boomer every seven-and-one-half seconds. In 2020, there will be approximately 120 million people in this country over the age of 50.

 The term *senior citizen* no longer applies to these naturally gray-haired men and women who spend more time exercising and staying fit than their parents did. They also have spent the first half of their lives shopping and, with that much practice, there is little likelihood their spending habits will change.

*Newton's First Law*
For every action, there is an equal and opposite reaction.

**Being the Shopper *First Law*:**
**For every consumer trend, there is an equally**
**powerful countertrend.**

In fact, for most of the adult life of the baby boomers, the United States has been in a growing economy. Since 1990, we have seen that the fastest growing age group of the boomers, the 45- to

54-year-olds, have the highest household income. They also spent more on consumer goods than any other age cohort. However, spending might soon slow. In fact, surveys conducted during the 1990s by both the U.S. Census Bureau and the Bureau of Labor Statistics reported declines in household income and spending between the 45-to-54 age group and those 55 to 64.

However, this is the baby-boom generation, and it is fair to predict that this "shopping 'till you drop" trend will continue, as the boomers age in a much younger way than did their parents. Unlike previous generations, most boomer couples are both wage earners and are well educated. They will continue to work and are expected to delay their exit from the labor force because they are healthier,

**Median Income (in $)**
**All Races and All People 15+**

| Age | Working Males | Working Females | Households |
|---|---|---|---|
| 15–24 | 20,825 | 18,960 | 27,689 |
| 25–34 | 34,218 | 27,953 | 44,473 |
| 35–44 | 41,560 | 30,471 | 53,240 |
| 45–54 | 46,674 | 31,981 | 58,218 |
| 55–64 | 46,752 | 30,282 | 44,992 |
| 65–74 | 48,185 | 33,276 | 28,147 |
| 75+ | 45,578 | 36,846 | 18,873 |

*Source:* U.S. Census 2000.

According to the U.S. Census Bureau, the median family income in the United States in 2000 was $42,100. Median income means that half of all households had incomes above $42,100 and half had incomes below that number. When we break down the data by age, you can see which groups have the greatest financial (and shopping) power.

---

**BOOMER WOMEN ARE EDUCATED**

Boomer women, in particular, are quite different from previous generations. For example, 28 percent of women ages 45 to 54 are college graduates, versus only 19 percent of women 55 to 64.

In addition, two-thirds of those college grads, ages 45 to 54, work full-time (and earn an average of $50,000 a year), versus less than half of similarly educated women 55 to 64 years old.

---

invigorated, and also have the need to accomplish more—especially because so many of them delayed marriage and still have financial responsibilities for their children and housing. Inheritances from their parents are also expected to be a windfall in paying off mortgages and buying high-ticket lifestyle items, including boats and second homes. Boomers will be entering their mid-50s and 60s with their household income undiminished. This significant change in demographic patterns will create huge shopping opportunities.

## The New Ethnic Mix: More than a Cultural Stone Soup

For many years, most immigrants coming to the United States were from Europe. In the year 2000, however, only 15.3 percent of immigrants were from Europe, with 25.5 percent from Asia, and 51 percent from Spanish-speaking countries. Present trends show a large influx from the Middle East and Caribbean areas. Foreign-born residents of the United States totaled 28.4 million, the highest percentage (10.4 percent of the total U.S. population) in almost 50 years. For marketers the impact is great: According to the *Funk & Wagnall's World Almanac*, total spending power of African Americans, Hispanics, and Asians will have increased by almost $300 billion by the year 2000. In 2000, income increased for African Americans by 5.5 percent, Hispanics by 5.3 percent, and remained static for all other groups including Caucasians. In this chapter, I explore the biggest trends among these racial groups that affect marketing and brand development.

## African Americans Are Younger

The population of African Americans (33.5 million in 2000) is generally younger than the total U.S. population, and is centered in urban areas, although suburban populations of African Americans are increasing. Purchasing power increased to $533 billion, an increase of 72.9 percent from 1990 (far outweighing the 56.7 percent increase in total buying power). Influenced by gains in income, education, and population growth, African Americans' share of U.S. buying power has jumped from 7.4 percent in 1990 to 8.2 percent in 1999, according to the Selig Center for Economic Growth at the Terry College of Business, University of Georgia.

This survey suggests the importance of adapting your advertising medium to reach African American consumers:

**African Americans and Advertising:**
**What Advertising Influences You?**

| Medium | African Americans | Non-African Americans |
|---|---|---|
| TV ads | 41% | 33% |
| Radio ads | 24 | 13 |
| In-store displays | 57 | 50 |

*Source:* Food Marketing Institute, *African American Grocery Shopper 2000.*

## Asian Population Will Grow from 4.5 Percent to 9 Percent of the Total U.S. Population

As reported in the 2000 U.S. Census, there are 12.7 million Asian/Pacific Islanders in the United States, totaling 4.5 percent of the population. Most (93 percent) of the Asian/Pacific Islander population is of East Asian origin: 24 percent Chinese, 18 percent Filipino, and 12 percent Japanese. Of the Pacific Islanders, 58 percent were Hawaiian. By the year 2050, the total Asian population in the United States is expected to reach 34 million, accounting for 9 percent of the total U.S. population.

Compared to the average of 51.7 percent of households in general, more Asian/Pacific Islander families (61 percent) are headed by married couples. Fewer than average (9 percent versus 12 percent) families are headed by a single mother, but a higher percentage (6 percent versus 4 percent) are headed by a single father. Families of the total ethnic group were slightly larger than non-Hispanic White families (3.8 members versus 3.1 members, respectively) and there was a higher percentage of larger families (5 or more members) compared to non-Hispanic White (22 percent versus 12 percent). Nearly 60 percent live on the West Coast, comprising 8 percent of the population there, and Asian/Pacific Islanders are more likely than non-Hispanic Whites to live in urban areas.

In 1999, Asian/Pacific Islanders' buying power rose to $229 billion, an increase of 102 percent over 1990 levels and greater than that of Hispanics (84 percent) and African Americans (73 percent).

## The Hispanic Population Is Diverse (Which Means Smarter Marketing)

In the mid-1980s, many companies recognized the potential growth of the Hispanic market (31 million people with $383 billion to spend in 1999) and began translating their advertising messages— word for word—directly into Spanish. Not understanding the differences between the origins of the Hispanic populations created more problems than sales. Braniff airlines launched its Spanish ad campaign urging customers to "fly in leather"—when translated, the ads instead told them to "fly naked." Perdue chicken's advertising slogan, "It takes a tough man to make a tender chicken," translated into Spanish became, "It takes a sexually excited man to make a chicken affectionate." A frozen food manufacturer used the word *burrada* to describe its burrito line, not knowing that the word was slang for "huge mistake." Marketing mistakes like these for the most part are in the past, but they underscore the importance of knowing your shopper before you try to sell them, and what can happen if you don't.

By 2025, the United States will have the world's second largest Hispanic population. In the 2000 Census, the U.S. Hispanic population totaled 35.3 million (12.5 percent of the total), with just over 20 million (58.5 percent) of Mexican origins. Just under 10 percent of Hispanics are Puerto Rican, 3.5 percent from Cuba, and 28 percent listed themselves as "other." Los Angeles, New York City, and Miami are home to over one-third of the total Hispanic population.

Just identifying these ethnic shoppers is not enough. On October 26, 2001, McDonald's, after a successful six-store test, rolled out four so-called Latin menu items in South Florida: a Cuban Sandwich (ham, pork, Swiss cheese, mustard, and pickles on Cuban bread), Latin McOmelet (ham, onion, tomato, butter, orange, spicy cheese), Dulce de Leche McFlurry dessert and pineapple-mango McNugget dipping sauce. McDonald's objective is clear—they want (and need) to attract the Latin customer to their stores. But is their strategy right?

Will the Hispanic, or Latin, family, especially in South Florida, want to go to McDonald's? Culturally, a Latin mealtime is a group event that includes family, coworkers, or friends. Does a table and seats for four meet this societal need? What about the menu? Who are these products designed for? In Cuban, Puerto Rican, and Mexican homes and restaurants, eggs are traditionally served with rice and beans. Bite-sized pieces of chicken are usually spicy and served on the bone (wing-style) with a tomato- or chile-based sauce. And many Latin foods are cooked in lard for more flavor.

My prediction is that these menu items will attract a few Hispanics and a few Anglos, and disappear in their current incarnation. McDonald's effort does, however, underscore the opportunity to develop a nationwide chain of Hispanic restaurants for Hispanic customers. McDonald's failed to *be* the Hispanic fast-food customer—

they stopped short of truly understanding this particular shopper's unique needs and desires. A good place to start research on this shopper is to study the extensive line of foods from Goya and the loyal customers who flock to them. This is one of the few brands that does not try to be all things to all people: It focuses closely on the needs and wants of the members of its market.

 If you want to develop products for consumers of different ethnic origins, know your shopper first. Observe how they buy, what products they prefer, and in what quantities they want them. How do they cook, and for how many people are they cooking? Digging deeper into the cultural habits and likes of a particular age or ethnic group will be more difficult than writing a bullet point on a marketing plan that identifies a target market. That, I promise. However, truly understanding the shopper will improve your chances of success.

# CHAPTER 3

# The Shopping Experience

The average consumer's supermarket experience entails walking up and down 44,600 square feet of aisles and passing about 34,000 different products. In analyzing various industry studies and data, I've calculated that the average supermarket trip in 2001 lasts only 22 minutes. The math is simple and the challenge enormous: The average product only gets one twenty-sixth of a second to attract our attention and say, "Buy me." Therefore, understanding the shopping experience is just as important as understanding the consumer.

In this chapter, I'll introduce Lisa, a typical shopper. Being Lisa means habitually preparing frozen foods for her two children, in spite of her desire to serve them healthy, home-cooked meals. And, as this story shows, being Lisa also means being persuaded by superior customer service.

*Five o'clock Tuesday evening couldn't come fast enough for Lisa. It had been a long and tiring day. In the clothing store by seven that morning to get ready for inventory, she had had her next-door neighbor, Marti, make sure that Lisa's two daughters, Sarah and*

*Lori, ate a good breakfast and were ready for school. The 40-year-old women became friends when Lisa moved back to Denver. Marti was also divorced and had one son, Sam, now eight. Both worked part time and depended on each other to watch the kids, go shopping, and create some semblance of a social and family life.*

*Lisa had agreed to watch Sam tonight, while Marti had a dinner date, and to make dinner for all the kids. As she drove home, she tried to remember what she already had on hand that she could prepare. On nights like this, she wished there was some kind of fast-food restaurant nearby that made healthy foods that the kids would actually eat. Since turning ten last March, Sarah, her older daughter, had started to gain weight. Lisa was sure the culprit was the high-fat, high-sugar school lunches, as well as the hours each night that Sarah spent sitting in front of her computer playing games and e-mailing her friends. She wanted to teach Sarah how to cook healthily at home, but there never seemed to be time.*

---

**Lisa's children are not alone: In 2000, almost half of children aged 9 to 17 prepared meals for themselves, an increase of 300 percent from 1988. According to Yankelovich Partners, there's a great potential for bringing to market easily prepared and healthy foods aimed at these young cooks.**

---

*Lisa felt guilty about not making the full-course dinners that her mother had made for the family while Lisa was growing up. Times had changed, and her Mom had never worked outside the home, or had to raise two children by herself. Lisa couldn't focus on what foods she had at home and decided to make a quick stop at the supermarket to pick up something for dinner.*

## How Shoppers Shop

Each week, the average shopper makes 2.2 visits to a supermarket and spends $91 in total. The amount spent ranges from $55 for one person to $137 for households of five or more people. Surprisingly, the overall number of weekly shopping visits has remained relatively constant for the past 15 years. Shoppers have more retail choices. As a result, the number of food stores shoppers visited per week climbed from 1.4 stores in 1995 to 2.7 stores in 2000. The question is: Are shoppers going to more stores because there are more retail destinations? Or are they being forced to double their shopping trips in order to find the values or services they want?

*As Lisa pulled into the supermarket's parking lot, she realized this was the first time she was visiting this store. For five years she had driven past this supermarket twice a day three days a week without stopping. She always shopped at the same store with Marti and the kids usually on Sunday nights.*

*As she entered the store, she became confused. In her regular store, the produce department and bakery were in the front. In this store, she walked right into the deli and prepared foods department. The deli was making fresh pizza that smelled great. She hadn't thought about buying any foods that were already prepared—usually, on nights like this, frozen foods were the fastest and cheapest. A mouth-watering display of freshly cooked chicken, fish, pasta, and all kinds of veggies was now before her, and she stopped.*

*She looked at her watch. It was already ten minutes to six, and the kids would be hungry. The foods looked good, but she wondered if they would like them . . . or would she just be wasting money? She was 10 minutes from home, a frozen dinner would take about 10 minutes in the microwave, and she already knew which ones were the kids' favorites.*

*"That broiled chicken with mushrooms and broccoli is fabulous!" The voice startled her and made her look directly into the eyes of a 50-something-year-old woman dressed in a chef's hat and an apron embroidered with her name, Chef Lillian. "I made it fresh myself, just an hour or so ago. Just three minutes in the microwave and your family will never know you didn't make it. And if you have any kids, come over to this side—these meals are designed just for*

*them. Not only are they the right size portions, with the colors and shapes kids like to eat, but they are tasty and low in fat and calories. I'll guarantee they will eat every bite."*

*It was as if this woman was reading her mind. Lisa had tried this type of food before, meatloaf and chicken on black plastic plates that looked fabulous, but tasted like shoe leather. She wasn't going to waste money again. The woman sounded so genuine that Lisa almost believed the guarantee. "What makes these so special?" Lisa asked her. Chef Lillian took her time and explained how all these foods were prepared from scratch right in the supermarket's own kitchen under her close supervision. These were her recipes and, as a former restauranteur and registered dietician, she prided herself on knowing what her shoppers (of all ages) liked.*

*She asked Lisa to wait a minute as she walked back into the kitchen and quickly returned with a plate full of assorted, hot, bite-sized samples for Lisa to taste.*

## A Desire for Better Customer Service

When asked by the Food Marketing Institute's *Trends 2001* survey what improvement shoppers would make to their primary store, the number-one recommendation was to improve customer service. As Lisa's story shows, superior customer service can make an enormous difference in reeling in harried shoppers. In addition, in the same survey, shoppers reported that, although they have continued to shop at their same primary grocery store for 9.3 years, they'd learned to supplement their unfulfilled needs at other stores. What if one store filled all of their needs? Busy mothers like Lisa would likely benefit from this one-stop shopping.

## Being Visibly Acknowledged

Arguably, the most significant current trend within the culture of shopping is the idea of visibly acknowledging your customers—

## THE EXPRESS LANE MYTH

As Lisa left the new supermarket, she found the checkout experience was also superior, as the deli had its own register. The checkout is an often overlooked area of customer service. Many stores try to remedy this with express lanes. Have you ever really thought about how ridiculous express lanes in supermarkets are? As a marketer, you want to satisfy consumers. A survey conducted by *Adweek* magazine reported that 53 percent of shoppers disliked supermarket shopping, and another 13 percent actually hated it!

Shoppers like Lisa enjoy shopping for food, what they hate is the checkout experience.

Why can't we fix the problem? The reason is that most supermarkets don't realize they have a checkout problem. They point proudly to their express lanes or their self-scan checkouts, and proclaim that they have fixed the checkout debacle.

Sure they have—for those shoppers who buy a bag of chips, a quart of milk, and a loaf of bread. The ones they lose money on.

It's the shoppers with full shopping carts that marketers should be worried about. These are the shoppers that feel like they are in hell every time they get to the checkout.

Here's the challenge for supermarkets: why not create special lanes for shoppers with full shopping carts only? Have the best cashiers at these stations, with two baggers, and offer shoppers a soft drink while they are checking out.

The result? Everyone who spends a lot of money will shop at your store, and enjoy it!

something that Chef Lillian did to catch Lisa's attention. Today's shoppers are unwilling to settle and are willing to take the time and effort to find better value, service, information, and products. Consumers want to be respected and appreciated.

As the baby-boom generation reached the height of their buying power, most retailers went out of their way to develop customer-service training programs. Boomers were born under the spotlight and, as a result, continue to demand attention. Some customer service training programs worked, but others (that turned employees into "associates" or, worse yet, "Stepford Clerks") quickly communicated that the employees' only skill was memorizing key phrases, driving would-be shoppers out of stores.

People want to be acknowledged, whether it's when they walk into a room, sit around the dinner table, go for a walk on the street, or shop in a store. We need acknowledgment of our presence. A nod, a wave, or a wink can make us feel a part of a community that values our existence and our contribution.

 **For retailers and brand managers to create a relationship with the shopper, they must think community, partnerships, and belonging, and reinforce this approach in their messages. Online communities, such as those being established by Yahoo and AOL, will prosper and the new fee-to-belong strategies for unbiased online information will take hold.**

The Internet and cable television have created unique opportunities to reach consumers in a focused and cost-efficient manner. In the brief time that these two new media have appeared on the marketing horizon, neither has evolved into the magic bullet for selling goods and gaining loyal consumers. That will change as the electronic plumbing and programming for Web sites and portals become smarter and learn to visibly acknowledge. For now, the bricks-and-mortar establishments still have the best chance of satisfying your brand's consumers if they pay attention to the details and satisfy shoppers' emotional and primal needs.

Isn't that what we do to our consumers and potential consumers each day? Wal-Mart has become the world's largest retailer based on some very simple premises. Value and efficiencies are at the top of the list, for sure. However, let's not ignore the impact of their greeters. Walk into any Wal-Mart and you'll see a human being happy to welcome you into their store. As busy and stressed as you may be, their greetings and smiles visibly acknowledge you and help to set your shopping mood and experience. They communicate to the shopper that Wal-Mart wants and appreciates his or her business.

Amazon.com also understands shoppers, and every marketer should be learning from them. I now buy twice as many books and CDs as I did before I became a loyal Amazon shopper. They send e-mails notifying me of new releases, or reminding me of old releases that I might have ignored. Each time I sign on, my list of recommendations reminds me just how many CDs or books I don't have. Amazon goes out of their way to thank me for my order, and remind me just how important my business is to them. Amazon also makes me feel special (and trusted) by allowing me to order easily. The 1-Click® technology addresses the most worrisome aspect of my life—not having enough time, as well as not wanting to deal with a cumbersome ordering procedure that has me clicking on a half-dozen pages and messages. Amazon visibly acknowledges me; even though I have never actually spoken to anyone at the company. And, in return, I give them all my book and CD business.

What will it take for other brands to build these kinds of relationships?

 **Customer service remains a top priority for shoppers. Today, with a surplus of stores competing for the same shoppers, superior customer service can make an enormous difference. You might not realize it, but your store policies—such as empowering employees to take the extra step—have a significant impact on customer service and your ability to build lasting relationships with your customers.**

These anecdotes from real-life shopper Peter Grazier illustrate how employee empowerment and customer service go hand-in-hand.

### The Cookie

In the spring of 1997 I visited a grocery store called Fresh Fields in Devon, Pennsylvania. It's about 30 minutes from my home, but I had heard that the company focused on healthy foods, and that interested me.

During my visit there, I sauntered by the bakery counter, when my eyes were drawn toward the cookies. As a recovering cookieholic, I really was not interested in buying any. However, as I yielded to temptation, I focused on the healthy ones, with fiber and such. I asked if they had any crumbs or samples I could taste.

The young man serving me was kind and unusually patient as he mused over my obvious buy–don't buy dilemma. Instead of crumbs, he simply gave me an oatmeal cookie to taste. He then suggested the luscious (and expensive) chocolate chip cookies beside them—he said they were really good. Proudly, I refused.

Somehow, he seemed to notice a twinge of doubt in my refusal, so he asked again. Again, I refused—although I desperately wanted to try them. He must have sensed my desire, because when I returned home and opened the package of oatmeal cookies, I found two chocolate chip cookies that he had secretly slipped into the package!

Today I am a regular shopper at Fresh Fields, because of the cookie incident and other similar acts of customer service. What I sensed immediately was that this company must foster a culture of empowerment that allowed this bakery employee (or *team member*, as they are called at Fresh Fields) to make an independent decision to satisfy, no, delight this customer.

### The Orange

Closer to my home is another very good grocery store, at which I shop when I don't have time to visit Fresh Fields. This store's products are more traditional, but their service is generally good.

*(Continued)*

For the last few months, however, I have been having difficulty buying oranges. More times than not, when I get to the checkout counter, the price for oranges will be wrong—usually higher. Correcting this is inconvenient and sometimes embarrassing when there is a line of customers behind me. I have mentioned this to the produce people, but the problem still exists. A couple of nights ago I confronted one of the produce people again about the pricing problem, and pointed out another obvious error. To their credit, they handled me well, and worked with me to correct the problem. It finally took a manager to make a phone call and straighten out the pricing.

While the manager was phoning the other store, I talked with the young man in produce. He said that these juice oranges weren't selling because the price was just too high (because of the pricing error). I asked him if he could change it, and he said no. He also knew that they would be throwing out the oranges soon if they didn't sell.

His frustration in not being able to correct such an obvious problem in his own department was evident.

**The Lesson**

I tell these two contrasting stories because they relate directly to customer satisfaction and profitability as a function of employee empowerment. Two good grocery chains have two very different approaches to management.

At Fresh Fields, every employee is aware of his or her impact on profit and is empowered to take independent action to maximize it.

The decision to give two expensive cookies to a customer is not an insignificant decision. It is a business decision that may influence the relationship between a store and its customer.

Unfortunately, it is a decision that most employees in traditionally managed organizations have no authority to make.

In summary: Customers and profits can be won or lost when employees are enabled to take ownership of day-to-day problems.

Peter Grazier is founder and president of Teambuilding, Inc., Chadds Ford, Pennsylvania, www.teambuildinginc.com.

# CHAPTER 4

# Defining and Meeting Your Shoppers' Priorities and Needs

## The Culture of Shopping

Starting with baby boomers (born after 1945), and through Generation X, several generations of consumers now have, on the whole, experienced unprecedented economic growth, an unending series of new product innovations (both in electronics and consumables), branding of everything, and seeing salaries and investments increase year after year. With this prosperity came a new lifestyle, called *shopping*.

## The Role of the Supermarket

Within this culture of shopping, the supermarket is a prominent player. According to the U.S. Department of Agriculture, in 2000, families spent 11 percent of their disposable income on food. Since the 1940s, the percentage of disposable income spent on food has been steadily declining in the United States, reflecting both the efficiencies of the food industry and the increasing prosperity of the economy.

The most recent Consumer Expenditure Survey from the Department of Labor indicates that 58 percent of food expenditures are on food consumed at home. For the average household, food spending is the third largest category, following housing and transportation.

The chart on page 45 shows who is most likely to do the food shopping, and how much time and money he or she spends there.

Understanding who the most frequent and lucrative shoppers are is one step, but is it important to know exactly what these consumers want from their supermarkets and preferred food brands? Find out from the experts—*Trends in the United States,* an annual consumer survey commissioned and published by the Food Marketing Institute (FMI). The objective of the survey is to measure the various levels of importance that consumers allot to various factors when choosing where to shop for their groceries.

The FMI analysis finds that a closer look at the top five features reveals that the most important factors are:

- A clean, neat store—rated very important more often by older shoppers (ages 65 and older) and women working less than 20 hours per week.

- High-quality fruits and vegetables—very important to all subgroups, but especially valued among the highest income households, in which 90 percent rate it very important. Generally, the importance of high-quality fruits and vegetables increases with the shoppers' age. Men, younger shoppers, and shoppers in the lowest income category rate this attribute lower.

### How Many Times Shoppers Go to a Supermarket or Grocery Store in an Average Week

| | One (%) | Two (%) | Three (%) | Four (%) | Five (%) | Six+ (%) | Every Two Weeks or Less (%) | 2001 Average |
|---|---|---|---|---|---|---|---|---|
| Total | 31 | 30 | 20 | 5 | 3 | 3 | 4 | 2.2 |
| **Gender** | | | | | | | | |
| Men | 28 | 32 | 22 | 3 | 3 | 4 | 5 | 2.3 |
| Women | 32 | 29 | 19 | 6 | 4 | 3 | 4 | 2.2 |
| Work 20+ hrs/wk | 31 | 31 | 21 | 5 | 4 | 4 | 2 | 2.3 |
| Work 0–19 hrs/wk | 28 | 28 | 17 | 6 | 4 | 1 | 5 | 2.0 |
| **Age** | | | | | | | | |
| 15–24 | 29 | 28 | 18 | 7 | 1 | 4 | 6 | 2.3 |
| 25–39 | 26 | 32 | 25 | 4 | 3 | 3 | 3 | 2.3 |
| 40–49 | 23 | 32 | 22 | 7 | 6 | 4 | 3 | 2.5 |
| 50–64 | 39 | 25 | 17 | 4 | 5 | 3 | 4 | 2.2 |
| 65 and older | 40 | 32 | 10 | 4 | 0 | 1 | 6 | 1.7 |
| **Income** | | | | | | | | |
| $15,000 or less | 24 | 29 | 16 | 14 | 4 | 1 | 10 | 2.2 |
| $15,001–$25,000 | 30 | 33 | 20 | 3 | 3 | 3 | 6 | 2.2 |
| $25,001–$35,000 | 33 | 30 | 21 | 5 | 3 | 3 | 5 | 2.1 |
| $35,001–$50,000 | 31 | 32 | 22 | 3 | 4 | 5 | 3 | 2.4 |
| $50,001–$75,000 | 33 | 33 | 20 | 5 | 4 | 3 | 2 | 2.3 |
| $75,001 or more | 29 | 26 | 25 | 8 | 5 | 3 | 3 | 2.4 |
| **Residence** | | | | | | | | |
| Urban | 33 | 29 | 20 | 5 | 4 | 5 | 3 | 2.3 |
| Suburban | 34 | 29 | 23 | 4 | 4 | 3 | 3 | 2.2 |
| Small-town | 29 | 33 | 19 | 4 | 3 | 4 | 5 | 2.3 |
| Rural | 29 | 33 | 20 | 7 | 3 | 0 | 7 | 2.0 |
| **Size of Household** | | | | | | | | |
| One | 40 | 28 | 10 | 4 | 2 | 3 | 9 | 1.9 |
| Two | 35 | 33 | 20 | 2 | 3 | 2 | 3 | 2.0 |
| Three–four | 27 | 31 | 25 | 6 | 4 | 4 | 3 | 2.4 |
| Five or more | 18 | 29 | 30 | 11 | 5 | 6 | 1 | 2.8 |
| **Type of Household** | | | | | | | | |
| With children | 22 | 29 | 30 | 7 | 4 | 5 | 2 | 2.6 |
| Aged 0–6 | 25 | 28 | 27 | 8 | 5 | 6 | 1 | 2.7 |
| Aged 7–17 | 20 | 28 | 31 | 8 | 5 | 5 | 3 | 2.7 |
| No children | 38 | 32 | 14 | 4 | 3 | 2 | 5 | 2.0 |

*Source:* Food Marketing Institute.

## Top Factors in Selecting Primary Supermarket

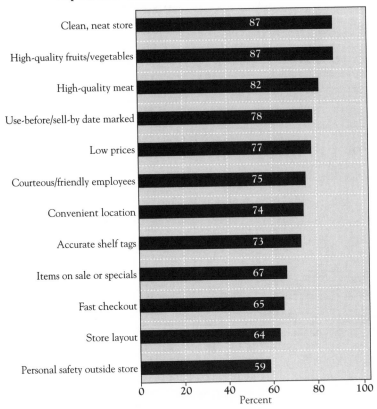

Source: Food Marketing Institute.

- High-quality meat—more often ranked very important by shoppers in the South. It also is important to women who work less than 20 hours per week.
- Use-before/sell-by date—more important to shoppers in the South. It is less important to men.
- Low prices—in comparison to 1999's survey, the importance of low prices has increased significantly. Low prices are especially important to larger households and younger shoppers.

**Importance and Performance**

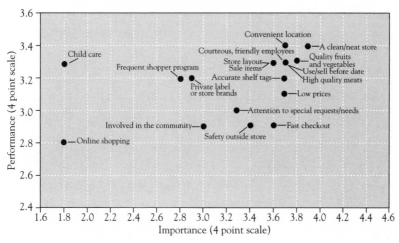

*Source:* Food Marketing Institute.

## What's Important to Consumers?

In their *Trends* survey, the FMI was able to visually plot the priorities of shoppers. By comparing the mean rating scores for importance and performance, retailers and brand managers can easily see where improvements should be made and which will be most important to shoppers.

To read the FMI survey chart, consider each of the four quadrants in terms of high or low importance and high or low performance or satisfaction. In the upper-right section, both importance and performance are high. These are features that are very important to shoppers and also where shoppers rate performance higher than average. For the categories in this quadrant, marketers should aim to maintain a high level of performance to meet customer needs. If these services were to slip, customers would notice and likely shop elsewhere. This analysis is based on the average shopper, however, and it is probable that if additional charts were produced for certain types of customers, the results might be different. For example, certain consumers, examined through specific demographics or shopping habits, may consider fast checkout or frequent-shopper programs more important and might rate performance differently.

## The Psychology of Shopping: A Consumer's View

Too often retailers rely on in-store gimmicks, instead of real merchandising, to build their business. It should not be just about traffic—the greater focus should be on building long-term relationships.

Many books have been written about the conscious and subconscious behaviors that make consumers buy. Some of these behaviors are tried and true, others more myth than reality.

With almost 40,000 products on supermarket shelves, each brand has to do its best to attract attention and turn itself into dollars at the cash register. Whether it is the color of packaging, music in the background, or location on the shelf, that makes the difference to consumers, retailers have to do whatever it takes to get more from each consumer visit.

What do your shoppers think about your merchandising? We polled our SupermarketGuru.com consumer panel and asked what got them to buy more, and how they felt about various tactics. Here are some of the responses:

- A huge frustration is end-of-aisle displays. They say the end-of-aisle displays imply, but do not mean, the products are on sale. Huge handwritten price signs are often misleading.

- When stores place complementary items together—like beer and pretzels, or baby food and diapers—they are playing on shoppers' impulsiveness, but most of our panel agreed this integrated merchandising makes items convenient. Who can resist the shortcake and whipped cream nuzzling the strawberries on your list?

- Parents dreaded the cereal aisle the most. The most expensive children's breakfast cereals are often placed at kids'-eye level (not adults'), and parents say that this is not fair.

*(Continued)*

- When it comes to the packaging, consumers are not fooled by *new* or *new and improved.* They know the terms can mean the product has just come out or has been made better, *or* it can mean a new color, new flavor, or just a tweak in the formula.

  When it comes to building relationships in this new era of consumerism, the most important element is honesty. Consumers are tired of shopping around looking for the best deal on the Internet; what they want is a reliable retailer who knows them, takes care of them, and wants their business.

  The food industry has given a great deal of lip service to customer satisfaction; the time has come to make our relationships with consumers the most important product we have.

## Cleanliness and Safety Are Number One

Food safety is the number-one reported concern of the over 2.5 million consumers who visited SupermarketGuru.com in 2000, and they don't place the responsibility to fix the problem solely on the USDA or FDA. Our consumer panel sees the responsibility divided: part government, part retailer, and part consumer. Last year, according to the Centers for Disease Control, there were 76 million illnesses, 325,000 hospitalizations, and 5,000 deaths from foodborne pathogens in the United States.

**When it comes to food safety, *being the shopper,* means understanding that people are fearful and don't want to die from eating a particular food. The proper listening to (and learning from) this consumer need is not limited to those who market beef and its related products, but for all consumables. The clear and easy-to-read expiration dates on chips, cookies, soup cans, and dairy products are as much a marketing tool**

as they are a must-have food-safety guideline. Currently, there are no federal guidelines for expiration or sell-by dates (except on certain baby foods and formulas), which gives brands the opportunity to enhance their relationship with shoppers by using large, easy-to-understand expiration dating. Shoppers want to know what they are buying, how long it will last in the package, how the product will taste, how to prepare it, and how to store any leftovers safely.

While thus far there have been no reported cases of foot and mouth or mad cow disease in the United States, the psychological impact of these diseases on the British and Japanese shoppers should be of concern to, and a warning to, U.S. marketers. Consumers in both the United Kingdom and Japan have greatly reduced the amount of beef they consume; some shoppers have eliminated it altogether. U.S. exports of beef to Japan (the number-one importer of U.S. beef) have practically ceased, resulting in a dramatic drop in the price of beef worldwide. Global food resources have been strained and, with the threat of additional breakouts, we can expect to see increased costs of manufacture, shipping, and packaging to prevent this disaster from reaching our soil. For the next decade, we will see meat prices (and meat advertising) increase, which will also drive consumers to find other allegedly safer and cheaper sources of protein.

---

*Clearly mark all foods with expiration dates that can be easily read, in standard English instead of manufacturing codes.*

---

## Packaging for Safety

While retailers and brands are doing everything they can to project an image of safety, the boost of real confidence and increased market share will come from new, smart packaging that can actively alert a shopper to a food safety hazard.

Two such examples are now in production; we can expect a lot more as DNA technologies allow us to isolate (and control) bacteria.

Fresh-Check® smart labels, produced by LifeLines Technology, are color indicators used to guarantee that a product has been in correct cold storage at all times. The labels are placed on the product immediately after processing. From then on, any time the temperature increases; the color of the indicator label gets irreversibly darker. When a shopper sees the product in the store, the labels will indicate the degree of exposure of that individual package to higher temperatures. Ensuring that a product has not been out of the safe temperature zone is important to reduce the risk of food-borne bacteria such as Salmonella, E. coli, Listeria, and Campylobacter. Consumers are demanding more information and they understand that, while most products have a use-by date, it doesn't rule out possible temperature mishaps along the way.

Toxic Guard, developed by Toxin Alert of Toronto, Canada, is a plastic wrap that, within minutes of coming in contact with bacteria, changes color and indicates that a particular bacterium is present. The possibilities of this technology are endless. Foods packaged using Toxic Guard would immediately indicate to the manufacturer the presence of bacteria before distribution. Consumers who store their leftovers in plastic bags with Toxic Guard will know if their food is still safe to eat days later. Beverage manufacturers could line bottles with Toxic Guard to see if water or unpasteurized juices are contaminated. Smart packages will become invaluable to consumers, who will be willing to pay the premium for peace of mind.

# PART TWO

# THE SHOPPING EXPERIENCE

CHAPTER

5

# e-Revolution
# Becomes e-Evolution

Is there a place for e-commerce in the hearts of food shoppers? The truth is that no one actually knows yet. According to most surveys, only 10 percent of shoppers have ever bought groceries online (as of October 2001). However, statistics like these fail to break out those shoppers who buy their weekly groceries online from those who purchase one pound of imported cheese once a year. Those consumers, who respond that they are not interested in buying their foods online, state that they want to see and touch what they are buying. Grocers are optimistic about the prospects, however, and, although most of the national online grocery shopping sites are now defunct, the food industry believes that a local, supermarket-based service is the answer.

With all that has been written since the demise of one promising grocery Web site, WebVan, in mid-2001, most marketers still seem to be missing the key lesson: It's about *being the shopper!*

Imagine two people standing at different ends of the cereal aisle. One wants to buy the healthiest cereal they can find, while the other wants to buy the largest box of cereal, regardless of brand or variety, at the cheapest price. You wouldn't try to merchandise or sell to them in the same way, would you?

Of course you wouldn't. However, when we take a look at the debacle of food in the world of e-commerce, it seems that we tried to do just that: lump together a selected group of consumers—upscale, time-crunched, 40-somethings—and treat them all the same, ignoring their basic needs.

*Basic Need #1.*   Consumers enjoy shopping for many foods. Shoppers like picking out produce and meats and baked goods and prepared foods. They hate buying toilet paper, paper towels, laundry detergent, and bottled water. The e-commerce model depended on selling the higher profit items that people want to buy for themselves and, in the long term, that just won't happen.

---

### THE FUTURE OF THE INTERNET . . . AND OF FOOD

There is no question that the Internet has changed the food world. Although you might be thinking that the biggest changes are in the way consumers buy (or will buy) their foods, I would suggest that the change is much more significant.

Today, about 1 percent of food sales are electronic, and the majority of these are transacted by telephone. Predictions are that by the year 2005, one-third of all food sales will be conducted electronically. In fact, a survey of 1,000 consumers, conducted by the Food Marketing Institute, found that 20 percent said they were either very likely or somewhat likely to try grocery shopping on the Internet.

In addition, the major impact of the Internet on our foods will be in the way the communications about food are handled—to both the consumer and to the trade.

Unfortunately, the quality of the content means less than the number of bytes. Consumers, or *clickers*, are beginning to become frustrated by the sheer amount of information that is repetitive. The

*(Continued)*

biggest opportunity remains with the search engines that can focus in on just the information that you want, and that somehow qualifies the content.

There is a downside to the seemingly unlimited storage capacity of the Internet: As we deluge people with too much me-too food information, we are creating a backlash that sends consumers to our supermarkets more confused than they were on their last shopping trip.

The need for consumer food (product, ingredients, recipes, etc.) and health information will continue to grow as the industry develops more functional foods, and continues to research the relationship between what we eat and how we feel and live.

Take a quick perusal of the Internet advice as it relates to trade food news, and you'll find that most information is the same; it comes from wire services.

Companies have chosen to use this communication tool to speed up getting to consumers and decision makers. Along the way, it picked up instant credibility. The nonvalidated benefit of appearing on a Web site seems as absurd as saying, "If it's in print, it must be true."

In the rush to sell products directly to consumers, in particular health supplements and diet miracle cures, so-called experts in health and nutrition are making unsubstantiated claims that would never be allowed on point-of-sale packaging. Sites offer news and information that is nothing more than company hype. Not only are we the victims, but also the perpetrators. We have to police our content.

*Basic Need #2.* E-tailers must understand that fulfilling 50, 60, or even 70 percent of a customer's shopping list is unacceptable. Forcing people to go to a store to buy a particular brand or size that is unavailable online just reinforces the shopper's questions about the benefits of buying online.

*Basic Need #3.*　Money talks, but just how it talks is important. Many users of WebVan's service told me that the major reason they were using the service was to get the $20 or $15 coupon savings on their order. Fine for an introduction—but week after week? The coupon also made them question just how much more they were spending on their groceries at WebVan's pricing levels as compared to their regular store.

Harry Wolhander, vice president of research for ActivMedia Research, was a guest on my syndicated radio program, *Shopping Smart*, in late September 2000. He told our listeners that it seems as if most grocers and brands agree that the Internet is the wave of the future when it comes to marketing and retailing to consumers. The good news, he said, is that this medium provides quick, 24-hour ordering capabilities, and allows customers to shop from the convenience of home.

 **The Food Marketing Institute's 2000 Survey, *The e-Tail Experience* finds that shoppers aged 25 to 34 are the most likely to shop for any type of products online. As this generation matures and, at the same time, the technology develops and becomes sophisticated enough to emit aromas and other kinesthetic influences, expect e-food sales to increase proportionately. For now, the Internet will remain a primary source for information, with shoppers continuing to purchase their groceries in a supermarket.**

What about the actual shopping experience that 90 percent of consumers say they want? Wolhander says that it is on the way. E-commerce will soon add the ability to scan a range of products that are similar to what you are looking for (just as walking down a supermarket aisle does), and will go a long way to bringing excitement back into online grocery shopping and promote impulse purchasing. One of the major drawbacks to ordering groceries online is that many shoppers make lists before heading to the market. The reality is that shoppers will point and click their way through the list with little regard to impulse items (that are usually flashing annoyingly

## ARE YOU LOSING YOUR HEALTHY-MINDED
## CUSTOMERS TO THE INTERNET?

Today, many shoppers are looking for the fountain of youth on the Internet. And, in their search, they may be shifting dollars from your stores and your bottom line. As the retail concept of whole-health solutions moves to reality for many retailers, it's critical to understand the breadth of your competition—the World Wide Web!

Shopping for healthy foods and supplements on the Web is easy. With just a few clicks, you can get to thousands of sites offering everything from dairy-free cheeses to potions that promise to turn back your biological clock. In fact, in just 0.24 seconds, my Google search engine found over 3,090,000 sites when I typed in the key words *health food*.

Forrester Research forecasts that by 2003 online grocery sales will reach $10.8 billion. Analysts suggest that almost a third of those dollars will be generated from nutritional foods and supplements.

There are some important distinctions between bricks-and-mortar operations and those in the virtual arena.

All foods sold on the Internet are subject to the FDA regulations for interstate commerce; but there is no proactive effort from the agency to monitor these sites. The FDA will handle complaints on a case-by-case basis but, with the enormous number of sites available, it is improbable that much more can be done with present staffing and resource levels.

The FDA and the FTC share the responsibility of regulating health claims made on the Internet. Certain statements, like "lowers cholesterol," might be perceived as labeling, and therefore subject to FDA regulations.

Other claims, like "increase your energy and cardiac output," could be perceived as advertising, and be subject to FTC scrutiny and regulation.

Companies can literally put anything on their Web pages to promote a product and, until they are caught, many consumers may get ripped off and even jeopardize their health.

*(continued)*

59

*(Continued)*

This is the opportunity to build a strong relationship with your customers. It is rather simple to make Web sites look professional and credible, but that doesn't mean that they truly are. The company behind the Web site will be integral to how successful a quest for healthy offerings will be.

Healthy foods have come a long way, and so have retailers like Wild Oats and Whole Foods who, in addition to selling us foods and supplements, have the resources to answer our questions and protect us.

These and other retailers evaluate products and verify product claims before the products appear on their shelves.

in the margins of the Web page), which virtually eliminates the possibilities of other products catching their eye, nose, or tastebuds, as frequently is the case in the bricks-and-mortar supermarket. The online experience is rather boring without those sensory cues that persuade shoppers to make impulse purchases.

## From e-Revolution to e-Evolution

So, where does e-commerce go from here? Back to the shopper!

*Meal-concept generation* is my formal marketing lingo for *making dinner* in a way that meets shoppers' needs, is fun, and uses technologies that now exist. Shoppers currently do their menu planning by walking down the supermarket aisles, clipping newspaper or magazine recipes and ideas, or learning from family and friends—or from whatever they can find and assemble quickly in their kitchens. The e-evolution phase of food marketing is about to change.

Imagine watching yet another broadcast of *The Godfather*, or *The Big Easy*, or *Casablanca*, or *Big Night*, or just about any other film you can name. There always seems to be a pivotal scene in a restaurant or around a dining-room table. You intently watch—and *bam!* You find yourself getting hungry. No problem! Don't even think about getting up from that chair or bed.

Just point your wireless remote control—or maybe your Personal Digital Assistant (PDA)—at your television screen, or, if it is too far out of reach, just say "dinner description." Either way works. A pop-up window appears on your screen with a complete description of the dinner being served in the movie. You can select each dish individually and access the recipe, history, nutritional information, and ingredient sourcing.

Want to customize the meal? Just say "my diet," and the screen will automatically show a recalculated version based on your preprogrammed individual nutritional desires—higher protein, more fiber, vitamins, herbs, lower fat, fewer calories—all are recalculated and appear in less than a nanosecond.

It gets even better.

Say "Tonight, seven o'clock, four people" and the device will automatically communicate with your refrigerator, freezer, and pantry to be sure you have the necessary ingredients. Something frozen? Don't worry; the thaw unit built into your fridge will have it thawed in time. If you are missing an ingredient, don't worry, the device will send an electronic order to your predetermined food-delivery service that will deliver your order just in time for preparation. At the appropriate time, your kitchen computer's electronic voice will find you—at home, in your car, or on the telephone, to remind you it's time to start the meal preparation.

Our stoves, ovens, microwaves, and blenders will be interconnected and recipe times and temperatures downloaded. No buttons to press or pots to watch. Soufflés are perfect, roasts tender, and even the most delicately blended Oriental soy-enriched pasta with tamarind sauce is foolproof. If all this *still* seems like too much work, or if you are just too busy to make the meal yourself, all you have to do is say, "Deliver it, tonight, seven o'clock, four people."

The way shoppers think about food acquisition will change. No longer will the weekly shopping trip be perceived as rigid or boring. Our culture will move to a more meal-oriented way of thinking,

## ARE BARCODES THE KEY AT RETAIL?

Pick up *Parade* magazine, *TV Guide*, *Forbes*, and many other glossy consumer magazines and what do you see? Barcodes!

The idea is simple—have consumers scan the code and everything they need to know about an advertised product will appear on their computer screen. Once again it sounds like Marketing 101—however, even if the technology worked perfectly, it's based on a flaw. The flaw is that consumers will be reading (or want to be reading) near their computer.

Sure, as the technology evolves, a wireless PDA device might make the location issue moot, but do you really think consumers want to read a Web site on a two-inch-by-three-inch screen?

Whether you see sense in this marketing ploy or not, it's here, and you had better be aware of it. Here's a primer on the three most popular applications, and how they fare.

**Barpoint.com** (http://www.barpoint.com) is a Web site and a Palm Pilot (wireless) Web-clipping application that lets you search for a product via its UPC barcode. After you type in the bar code, you can receive extended information about the product including manufacturer contact info, product reviews, price comparisons, where-to-buy info, auction site searches for the product, and so on. This added-value information is not created by the company but obtained through third-party relationships (i.e., clickthebutton.com for comparison shopping).

I did a few barpoint.com searches on books, CDs, software titles, toys, and it didn't do too well identifying most of the exact products. In the company's defense, it is a *huge* task to enter all of the UPC codes for *all* the products out there.

Go to Radio Shack, and you can pick up a free **CueCat,** www.cuecat.com, which is a cat-shaped bar-code scanner that is (according to published product reviews) next to impossible to make work with your PC. Digital Convergence is the company that offers the hardware and software through partners such as Radio Shack and *Wired* and *Forbes* magazines.

The magazines run ads containing bar codes. After swiping your CueCat over them, it points your Web browser to the product or

*(Continued)*

manufacturer's Web page. Even if the CueCat actually worked well, there are a million problems with the concept. As we said before, do you really want to be reading a magazine while sitting at the computer? How hard is it to find a company's Web site anyway? Wouldn't it be wiser for a company to put Web addresses in their advertisements?

The real story about CueCat is that Linux hackers are hitting their local Radio Shack for the free readers, wiping out the memory chips on the device, downloading new (hacked) drivers to make the Cue-Cat work with their favorite database programs, so they can start cataloging things like their CD collections, libraries of tech books, and the like.

The company also offers a TV/computer/CueCat hook up, so that you can receive audio bar codes to activate your Web browser. The problem is that you need a special cable to hook up your computer to your television.

**deBarcode** (http://www.debarcode.com) is an Internet directory service specializing in bar codes and universal-resource identification. Given the bar code of a product, deBarcode will locate its maker's Web site. Basically low frills, they are taking a more grassroots approach to gathering UPC codes, by encouraging manufacturers to enter their product into their database. For manufacturers to participate, they must install deBardcode software on their Web servers, so that the URLs of the products would be correct.

Of the three companies, I believe Barpoint.com has the best chance of success, but there are other companies competing in this space as well. The idea that you'll be able to walk into a supermarket or other retailer with your cell phone or PDA, swipe a barcode, find the lowest price on- or offline and buy it at that moment is pretty interesting.

As the technology becomes cheaper and smaller, the challenge will be selecting the information that consumers want and need—and how that information affects the distribution channel and how a consumer chooses a product. What about real-time stock pricing on the company offering a particular brand of electronics and pricing? Sure, real-time price comparisons may be a killer application, but what long-term effect will it have on branding and building relationships?

which will be a valuable tool for better nutrition and will add more excitement to our meals.

## What about Those Kitchens?

The smart kitchen of the future is an extraordinary concept. Refrigerators, cupboards, and built-in scales that will all calculate use and automatically deliver staple foods to our home are the wave of the future. A delivery model based on Streamline's concept of

---

QUICK FACTS FROM CYBERDIALOGUE'S
AMERICAN INTERNET USER SURVEY 2000

The average Internet user will spend 63 million seconds, 23.5 months, or 5.3 percent of their lives on the Internet during their lives. Nine and one-half of those months will be spent using e-mail.

More than 40 percent of online adults (24.3 million) have changed their impressions of brands based on information they receive via the Internet; this figure is up 66 percent from 1.6 million in 1998.

Online shoppers note that cars are the product most likely to have brand names influenced by the Internet (21 percent), followed by airlines (20 percent), investments (13 percent), and household items (12 percent).

Manufacturer and comparison-shopping sites are most commonly cited reasons a brand impression had changed (70 percent and 69 percent, respectively).

Twenty-four percent of those shopping for vehicles online state that information found on the Internet led to the purchase of a different brand of car than that which they had considered.

Fourteen percent shop for both travel and insurance online.

Forty-two percent of those who shop online now report that online information has changed their impressions of brands, up from 35 percent in 1998.

*Source:* AIUS consists of in-depth interviews with 1,000 Internet users and 1,000 nonusers.

installing double-sided refrigerators and storage compartments will allow secure deliveries when the shopper is not at home.

A computer screen, located on our refrigerator door or on other appliances, will let us know when our inventory of certain products is running low. A message will advise that, in two days, we will run out of milk, and ask us if we want it delivered or if we will pick it up.

When we do go to the store, our PDA will replace our shopping list, recipe ingredients, coupon organizer, and nutrition information. As we walk down the aisle, information (and e-coupons) will appear. Just a click and that product can be comparison shopped and, if chosen, ordered. The acquisition choices are the shopper's as well—put it in the cart, pick it up at the checkout (already bagged and paid for), or have it delivered.

**Every industry needs to thinking about, and imagining, its future on the Internet, and how it could improve its customers' experiences. According to Forrester Research, the consumer side of the e-commerce opportunity is a market of $107.3 billion. In 2002, we will continue to see e-commerce shakeouts. It's not a sign that consumers are not willing to buy products and services online. Rather, it shows that we are not perceiving shoppers' wants and needs.**

## Before There Was e-Commerce, There Was Cable Television

Buying food online will work for some shoppers. However, let's remember that, as we move into this new arena of understanding how shoppers buy, there are lots of other venues to consider.

One of the most successful venues is cable television, with QVC at the head of the pack. It's a lot more than the pots and the pans . . . or even the automatic hot dog makers. QVC (now reaching over 68 million households) has sold over a million units of food products in 2000. Brands like Rao's Sauce, Mrs. Prindable's Apples,

Millie's Meals, Flossie's Funnel Cakes, and Chesapeake Gourmet have all found success selling products on QVC.

One reason that QVC has done so well is that they really want to sell food, and they asked consumers directly what they should be selling. In 1995 and 1997, they launched search tours across the country, not for new on-air talent, but for new food products. They've taken an active role in these local events and produced live remotes at the Taste of Chicago, Festival of the West, Gilroy Garlic Festival, and the New York State Fair. Some of their top-selling products include Cajun Marinade Injector, Junior's Cheesecakes, Kansas City Steaks, and Better than Bouillon.

QVC has successfully demonstrated that having five or ten minutes on air to talk and demonstrate a product will help it sell. Add some lights, pizzazz, and electronic wizardry, and it's not too different from an in-store sampling for millions. It's a food-marketing model that, in fact, brand managers would do well to study. QVC's sales approach (especially Bob Bowersox's food show, Sundays, noon

---

### FOODS SHOPPERS BUY ON QVC

- Mrs. Prindable's Apples and Gourmet Treats (13 pieces): 9,000 units were sold in 15 minutes on 12/10/98, at $30.

- Millie's Meals Low-fat Dry Soup Mixes (12 pack, 4 to 6 servings each): 4,416 units were sold in 11 minutes on 8/30/98, at $23.25.

- Virtually Hull-Free Microwave Popcorn (24 pack): 3,104 units were sold in 10 minutes on 10/18/98, at $14.50.

- Chesapeake Gourmet Jumbo Lump Crab Cakes (12 3-oz. cakes): 3,002 units sold in 10.5 minutes on 12/4/98 at $49, 1,812 units sold in 12 minutes on 12/10/98, at $49.

- Flossie's Funnel Cakes Mix Kit (2 24-oz. packages, one ring, one funnel): 5,792 units sold in 12 minutes on 1/10/98, at $16.25, 5,009 units sold in 8.5 minutes on 2/7/98, at $16.25, 5,048 units sold in 9 minutes on 10/11/98, at $16.25.

to 1 P.M.) understands consumers of all ages and socio-economic levels, and how to communicate effectively with them. QVC's hosts and presenters make shoppers a part of their program, and in return, shoppers call up and buy. It's one of the best examples of effective visual, auditory, and kinesthetic food selling.

Just how effective? Specialty and gourmet foods are the most popular on the network. This comes as no surprise, as cravings for rich, decadent products are ideal for impulse sales. For the 1999 Super Bowl, QVC scheduled a one-hour special to sell an assortment of products, including Philly Steak Sandwich Meat (3 pounds for $29), Virtually Hull-Free Microwave Popcorn (24 pack for $14.50), and Maryland Crab and Seafood Cakes, among others. Super Bowl Sunday has become a major food-sales event for supermarkets, typically focusing on nachos, beer, and cheeses; one of QVC's best selling products was a frozen seafood sampler (15 3-ounce portions for $50).

 **Electronic food retailing on television and the Internet reminds us of the importance (and effectiveness) of good product merchandising. The effectiveness of selling foods on cable television is a great lesson for marketers on how to entice customers in different venues. This flexibility and inventiveness will separate the companies who survive from those who don't survive during this retail evolution.**

# 6

# Identifying
# Your Shopper

**B**eyond demographics, each shopper has a unique approach to spending money and selecting brands. In this chapter, I focus on helping you discover what type of shopper your brand's main target should be. By discovering your main target, you can customize the venue for these shoppers, reeling them in, and making them loyal customers.

## Does Your Brand Connect with These Different Shoppers?

In this section, I introduce Raphael, a young family man and restaurateur, whose shopping needs are oriented to saving money. His wife, on the other hand, is attracted to different brands based on friends' recommendations, packaging, and her own impulsiveness. You'll learn the differences in their shopping personalities in a short quiz later in this chapter.

*As he circled the supermarket aisles during his weekly shopping trip, Raphael thought about how he could never quite define what a brand was. In his family's restaurants, he knew that putting their family name and logo on everything he could was important, because customers memorized and remembered it. However, each time he went grocery shopping, the thousands of brands lining the shelves just seemed to run together. All the colors and shapes became meaningless to him, and confused his choices instead of clarifying them, except for the store's own brand. That, he thought, was great marketing. Hundreds of products all with the same basic design and color scheme in every department selling at lower prices, and always placed directly to the right of the best-selling brand. It was easy to compare.*

*Geri, his wife, sometimes bought the store brand and sometimes the national brand. He wondered why she didn't always buy the cheaper one. Whenever he asked her about it, she became flustered (almost embarrassed) and couldn't give him a good answer. Geri said that the products tasted different; other times she said it was because it was a brand that her mother had used and she knew it was reliable. At times, it was because Victoria, their next-door neighbor and her friend, recommended it.*

Raphael is not alone in his feeling that we're deluged by brands. The Center for a New American Dream, in Tacoma Park, Maryland, reports that before an American child enters first-grade, he or she will have soaked in 30,000 advertisements. James McNeal and Chyon-Hwa Yeah, in their study *Born to Shop*, report that at six months, the same age at which a child is starting to emit simple sounds like "ma-ma," he or she is already forming mental images of corporate logos and mascots.

Raphael is also not alone in selecting the store brands. According to the Private Label Manufacturers Association, one-in-five products purchased in grocery outlets is a store-brand product. Store-brand sales now exceed $40 billion per year. However, that hasn't stopped consumers' unconscious absorption of brands and logos. Brands are everywhere. Clothing, electronics, computers, pens, kitchen utensils, and cars—just about everything that a shopper comes in contact with—have brand names and logos prominently featured. While Raphael consistently chooses the same lower-cost brands, other consumers, like his wife, buy brands and logos in order to present a certain image to the outside world, or based on the reputation and quality that they stand for. Some of these customers just accept the logo as part of the overall product.

A brand image is powerful and, at times, uncontrollable. The shopper's perceptions about a brand are stored in his or her memory, and are just waiting to be called up when needed to make a decision. The brand image is developed by a host of criteria, most of which is made up from associations with prior personal experiences, advertising, news reports, and even hearsay.

What images and feelings do you experience when you read this alphabetical list of brands?

Coca-Cola

Dom Perignon

Ferrari

Firestone

Microsoft

Nike

Playboy

tic tac

Tylenol

Which ones made you hungry or thirsty? Which ones fill you with desire to acquire? Which ones make you angry? Which ones make you smile?

Consumer perceptions of brands are multidimensional and, all too often, brand managers forget just how important and sacred the care of their brand is. The life of a brand manager on a typical

Consumer Packaged Goods (CPG) product can be as short as a few months, or as long as 20 years. There is no rule that says how long an individual should work on a particular brand: No matter how mature or how new the product or person in that position, brand-marketing people seem to be rotated on brands with too little thought given to their impact on the brand. Their primary focus should be on the product, changing it in some way to augment its signature value; or on the advertising, in an attempt to grow the sales or profits.

A prime responsibility of brand marketers is to take ownership and be the caretaker of your brand. Your ultimate goal is to leave the brand better than you found it, and to enhance its relationship with shoppers. This responsibility rests with everyone in an organization—it should be the primary responsibility of the CEO, as well as the marketing, production, operations, and administrative teams. The brand belongs to every shopper and every employee who works on it; everyone has a stake and responsibility for its health and well-being.

A shopper's relationship with your brand is built on honesty, trustworthiness, reliability, and predictability. Brands are created from nothing as are their personalities and attributes. Problems with brands happen when the brand manager is not paying attention or gets lazy. Every time a brand changes its image—whether through its advertising, packaging, logo, spokesperson, ingredients, and/or slogan—the relationship with the shopper changes. Uncertainty enters the relationship, and shoppers take a step back to see just what is going to happen, while waiting for the reassurances that nothing will alter the relationship they currently enjoy.

It is that relationship with the shopper that is all-inclusive and comprehensive. Positive relationships are based on human values: honesty, integrity, reliability, and trustworthiness. Successful brands add a personality to these values. Wendy's Dave Thomas brand added a bit of wit. Apple Computer brand adds innovation. Grey Poupon mustard brand adds style. Tiger Woods and Michael Jordan, the brands, have all of these, and a bit of charm as well. In 1996, *Financial World* magazine estimated that the Coca-Cola brand name was worth $45 billion, the Gillette brand $10 billion. Brand image is a combination and balance of functional and symbolic brand beliefs.

Your brand image might contain all of these elements, but if they are not communicated well and the shopper doesn't hear them, your brand will not be successful. Good communication has to be at the core of a meaningful brand relationship. Communications control the brand, and good communications enhance the brand by consistently communicating the brand's values and messages.

---

*There is no such thing as product loyalty*
*or trademark loyalty, only brand loyalty.*

**—Larry Light, Chairman of the**
**Coalition for Brand Equity**

---

In one of the earliest papers to investigate branding, Burleigh B. Gardner and Sidney J. Levy suggested, in a March–April 1955, *Harvard Business Review* article entitled "The Product and the Brand," that shoppers selected a particular brand when the clusters of values represented by a brand matched the customer's rational and emotional needs, thus enabling them to reinforce and communicate aspects of their personality.

In 1955, "you are what you buy" was little more than conjecture and hypothesis. In 2002, it is truth. In their recommendations, Gardner and Levy concluded that management needed to understand two basic points about brands:

1. *A reputable brand persists as a stable image through time.* The ideas people have about it are not completely malleable, not idly swayed by one communication and then another. If the public believes that a certain brand is of inferior quality, or that another is "on the skids," or that some other has all the latest improvements, these beliefs are not usually modified very rapidly. Such reputations are built through time, frequently in ways that management overlooks.

2. *It is rarely possible for a product or brand to be all things to all people.* It may be most desirable to sell to the most people, but hardly anyone can sell to everyone. Some brands have very skillfully built up reputations of being suitable for a wide variety of people, but in most areas, audience groupings will differ, if only because there are deviants who refuse to consume the way other people do.

The controversial introduction of New Coke didn't kill the Coca-Cola brand, but a scare of tainted product in Belgium left the world's number-one brand tarnished and damaged in Europe for years. In part, this incident led to the resignation of the company's president for his public mishandling of the brand's image and trust. Firestone's multigenerational-strong brand franchise was destroyed overnight with news reports of faulty tires causing deaths on highways, made worse by the company's inept press interviews and seeming lack of concern for the lives lost. Store-level tampering with Tylenol capsules could have destroyed a brand and company, but instead built a stronger and more trustful relationship with shoppers, when the company immediately recalled all of their products and their president announced that he had committed all their resources to the safety of consumers.

Shoppers have the information and news sources at their fingertips that Gardner and Levy could not have even imagined some 50 years ago. Brand loyalty and brand equity are simply measures of how well we're communicating. And, while megabrands may seem impenetrateable, they are as fragile as the latest news report makes them. Finally, in today's world, it is the Internet—and the opportunity for interactivity therein—that makes communication with the brand a more important element in marketing that it has been in the past.

Think of your brand as an egg, and you will start to understand the dynamics of a shopper's relationship with your brand. An egg has been called the world's most perfect package. It has a shell that allows air to pass through while protecting and nurturing a life, and when subject to equalized pressure on all surfaces, is unbreakable. However, take that egg and gently hit it with a fork, and it easily cracks open. In the lifetime of your brand, you should recognize that your brand will be cracked wide open a number of times for varying reasons. How the shopper reacts to those cracks will be based on their ongoing relationship with the brand. How you handle the cracks will be based on how well you understand your brand's relationship with the shopper.

 **The quality or, more accurately, the *perceived* quality of your brand is not about product—it is about the shoppers' judgments about your brand's overall excellence or superiority. Shoppers will be willing to expend more energy in processing information about a brand with whom they have a good relationship than those with whom they have little or no relationship. They have nothing to lose by ignoring a brand that is not included in their lives. It is also fair to say that well-known brands exhibit more developed brand associations than do unfamiliar ones.**

> *As they walked the aisles filing up their shopping cart, Raphael turned the cart down the paper-goods aisle. This was the aisle he most hated. He had tried repeatedly to bring home paper towels and toilet paper from the restaurant, but Geri refused to use it. She had tried the paper towels once, but said they didn't work as well as her brand, Bounty. "The quicker picker upper"—he recalled the slogan from their television commercials, but didn't really think there was much difference among brands of paper towels. Geri reached over to the Bounty towels and selected a three-pack. She called Raphael over to show him a new product—folded Bounty paper towels in a box—and asked him if he would like a box to put in the garage, instead of the roll he usually had on his workbench.*

As Raphael's aversion to Bounty towels shows, paper products are a challenging product to brand. In this case and others, nothing

| Shoppers Want Brands To | Marketers Want Brand Tools To |
|---|---|
| Help process needs | Differentiate between brands and products |
| Organize their lives | Position their brand |
| Retrieve information from memory | Extend brands |
| Aid in purchase decisions | Create positive attitudes and feelings |
| Reinforce purchase decision | Suggest attributes and benefits |

is more important for a brand than to develop and nurture a relationship with its shoppers. It's crucial to separate your needs, and to start looking at your brand and its brand tools (or associations) in the way in which a shopper does. The process will help you focus your messages and enhance the relationship between your brand and shoppers.

 **According to the Coalition for Brand Equity, as brand loyalty goes up, consumers grow less sensitive to changes in the brand's price. They also report that loyal customers are less likely to be sensitive to competitive promotions—driving down the brand's marketing costs. Frequent price promotions also reduce brand loyalty, while high advertising spending, price, distribution intensity, and good store image are related to high brand equity.**

Raphael's story also shows the delicate balance needed with brand extensions, using the example of Bounty's towels in a box. Similarly, one of Nabisco's leading brands is Oreo, and it is a perfect example of how brand extensions can increase shopper excitement and sales. From the cookie's invention in 1912, until 1975, the cookie basically remained unchanged to the eye of the shopper. Then, Double Stuf was introduced, and the company found that not only did the product increase consumption among current consumers, but also brought new users (many of whom had not eaten an Oreo since childhood) back into the brand. Many industry pundits questioned even more brand extensions. Are too many Oreos a bad thing? Obviously not. The shelves today are lined with successful Oreo extensions: Original Oreo Chocolate Sandwich Cookies, Fudge Covered Oreo, Mini Oreo Chocolate Sandwich Cookies, Reduced Fat Oreo Chocolate Sandwich Cookies, Oreo Double Stuf Chocolate Sandwich Cookies, and Chocolate Creme Oreo Sandwich Cookies.

Campbell's is known for its red-and-white cans of condensed soups. Over the years, Campbell's has attempted to move beyond the can into glass jars, paperboard containers for both dried and wet soups, and even to the frozen food case with tubs of soup and combo packs that married microwavable hot dogs and sandwiches with a cup of soup. Regardless of taste, price, or convenience, shoppers just didn't seem to want these other brand extensions from Campbell's.

A key lesson from the cases of Bounty and Oreo *versus* Campbell's is that the successful brand extensions involved creating new products that are placed alongside the core brand. In contrast, the Campbell's products were scattered all over the store, in places like the dairy and frozen case, where shoppers had to think twice about the brand's relevance in these unusual locations.

 **Be the Shopper** Effective brand extensions should do more than just add incremental sales to the company. They should show the shopper how a brand is evolving with consumer needs, and give the consumer both new and relevant information that is relative to the parent brand. A shopper's positive experience with a brand extension should create a stronger belief in, and relationship with, the parent brand. A negative experience will also chip away at that brand's image and have the shopper questioning their existing relationship, opening opportunities for competing brands to lure shoppers with their promise of trustworthiness and stability.

> *The influence of brand extensions on the parent brand is*
> *important to understand because they may change its core*
> *beliefs and thus either enhance or jeopardize its positioning.*
> —Daniel A. Sheinin, "The Effects of Experience
> with Brand Extensions on Parent Brand Knowledge,"
> *Journal of Business Research*

## Why Does a Shopper Choose a Particular Brand?

Even before a shopper makes out a shopping list or enters a store, the decision processes associated with evaluating, buying, consuming, and discarding products for personal consumption are present. As in the case of Raphael and Geri, some shoppers are malleable, some are not. Sometimes, there are influences that marketers don't even consider. We know from *The Wirthlin Report*'s research that Americans are conscientious comparison shoppers. The majority (87 percent) of those surveyed say, "Before I make a major purchase, I spend a lot of time finding out as much information as I can about which brand is best."

> *Geri steered the cart down the dairy aisle to pick up a quart of*
> *orange juice. Raphael's now-constant questioning of why she bought*
> *what was wearing down her patience. She bought one quart of*
> *orange juice every week from the same dairy case. It was the last*
> *aisle she shopped and, by the time she reached it, her patience and*
> *comparison-shopping skills were gone. She realized, for the first*
> *time, that this was another product whereby she didn't notice other*
> *brands or their prices.*

If you were the marketer of orange juice, how could you get a tired, harried shopper to notice your brand, yet alone purchase it? What would it take to get a shopper to desire more information about the orange juice category? How would you get him or her to consider an alternative brand? What is it about Geri's current brand

Typically, shoppers follow these five simple steps for each purchase they make:

1. Recognize the need for a product or service.
2. Search and gather information about the product or service.
3. Evaluate the information and alternatives available.
4. Decide to purchase.
5. Postpurchase behavior.

that has her so satisfied that she doesn't feel the need to even compare prices?

Within each of these five steps, there are influences (external, environmental, and internal) that add relief or anxiety to the shopper's decision-making process.

External forces are imparted by the values, norms, and beliefs of other people. They can manifest as a cultural bias—for example, believing that women are better food shoppers than men, or that all African Americans and Latinos are lactose intolerant, and that all women prefer white wine. Societal influences, such as occupation, education, or income are external forces that can move a shopper from one brand or category to another—as a shopper's income grows, for example, he or she might be more inclined to purchase pricier items like fresh fish instead of frozen fish. The personal service and relationship with the fish man might make the shopper feel better than average, thus justifying the higher cost.

Group influences also are among the strongest factors that can influence external decision-making factors. Neighbors, friends, families, coworkers, and supervisors, all comprise different behavioral groups that may add stress to a shopper's simple purchasing decisions. A boss who recommends a variety of wine will probably have more influence than a visiting in-law who brought the same wine as a gift. A friend on a diet who lost 15 pounds, and suggests a particular brand of yogurt, will probably be listened to more than an overweight neighbor suggesting the same brand.

Most shoppers laugh when I advise them to never go shopping when they are hungry, cranky, in a great mood, or in a bad mood; they will always ask me, "What time is left to shop?" My answer is that it depends on where they choose to shop. Environmental or situational influences on shoppers are the easiest to identify and control. It's why convenience stores can charge a higher price than supermarkets. Or why being on a beach in 90-degree weather means you won't mind paying $2 for a 10-ounce bottle of cold water. It's why shoppers will spend a Saturday morning pulling enormous packages off pallets at Sam's Club, instead of purchasing more manageable portions at their local supermarket. When a shopper is in the right frame of mind and prepared for these environments and situations, the experience and decisions are easy. Unprepared for this shopping experience, the event becomes painful, resulting in bad decisions such as being forced by the pressure of the environment to allegedly save by buying a five-gallon tin of olive oil that is on sale, in spite of the fact that the shopper consumes less than one liter every six months. Making brand decisions is tougher on a shopper than most marketers would like to believe, which is why it's important for us to discuss and understand each of these influences. The brand decision in some aisles may only take a split second to process and, in others, may require a few minutes of comparison shopping. Understanding the motivation of a shopper, combined with his or her internal personality and lifestyle needs, will help marketers focus their efforts to a certain extent. The external, or societal, influences on selecting a brand are just as important.

## External Influences: How a Group Can Influence a Brand Purchase

In sociology, we learn that an individual's set of basic values, beliefs, norms, and associated behaviors are learned in groups. Each shopper belongs to many groups: family, school, work, spiritual, and social, to identify but a few. On every shopping trip, influences from all these groups can play a part in making a buying decision.

Marketers cannot ignore that people are often the most powerful sources of buying influence. Word of mouth is, after all, the oldest form of advertising.

What about family members and spouses? Among married respondents in a 1999 survey conducted by *Wirthlin* on buying influences, both men and women agree that the wife has more influence on selecting a restaurant, deciding which brand of clothing to buy, and where to shop. Women also usually pick out the breakfast cereal, although 29 percent said children have a lot of influence over the decision in this category. Both sexes recognize that husbands take the lead when selecting a computer or a new car. Auto dealers take note: The woman's influence on car buying is not as insignificant as some would think; 58 percent of husbands say their wife has "a lot" of influence. Other decisions are shared evenly. Both spouses feel they have an equal say in choosing a vacation destination or which TV show to watch.

Some group influences are learned over time and, in many circumstances, have long-lasting effects on the behaviors of an individual. As an example of group influences, consider how marketing and salespeople react to shoppers.

Many people influence brand purchases. The newspaper food editor, television chef or correspondent, cookbook author, and even favorite talk-show celebrity are all food-brand opinion leaders. The brands they buy (or endorse) affect a shopper's decision. These opinion leaders are able to exert their influence on shoppers because of their special place in society. Their influence can be based on their skills, knowledge, personality, or just prominence. Marketers have begun to understand the importance of observing and tracking what these opinion leaders do and say about their own brands and those of their competitors.

Too often, though, brand marketers don't take the time or have the interest to really understand these opinion leaders and their

At age 64, my mom had to buy a new automobile by herself for the first time since my dad had passed away. I asked her if she wanted me to help her, and she answered that she needed to learn how to do these types of things by herself. She had decided on the type of car she wanted and went to a Chrysler dealer nearest her home. She approached a salesperson and told him that she wanted to buy a Chrysler Le Baron convertible. He looked at her, asked her to sit down, and told her that it wasn't the right car for her. It was noisy, had a small back seat, and, if the top wasn't secured properly, would leak. She insisted that she wanted that car, and said that she had never had a convertible and wanted one now.

He got up and asked her to follow him, and brought her over to a sedan on the showroom floor. "This is the best car for you," he said. My mother thought it was an "old-fart" car, was insulted, and left.

She visited another Chrysler dealer, further from her home, and went to another salesperson hoping for a different experience. When she told him what she wanted, he responded by saying that he wished his mom was that cool. She is now 79 and on her sixth Chrysler convertible (now Sebring), all purchased from the same salesperson who didn't have the cultural or group bias that led him to believe that older women don't drive convertibles.

Some group influences are ingrained and don't change. I doubt if that first salesman has ever sold a convertible to a woman over 60 or ever will. Other group influences can be temporary—called on in particular circumstances, and ignored in others. For example, purchase behaviors at lunch with colleagues may be different than those with your family.

needs, and too often find themselves lamenting a story or review that may have fractured their brand relationship with shoppers.

Most shoppers are not consciously aware of how their purchases are influenced. But by asking, "What source influences your buying decision the most?" *The Wirthlin Report* was able to learn something about the kinds of sources people deliberately seek out when actively considering a purchase. Not surprisingly, their survey finds that television has become the primary news source for Americans. Over half of those surveyed (58 percent) say they get their news mostly from television, evenly divided between network and cable television. Newspapers are the primary news source for about one-fourth (23 percent) of all Americans, followed by radio (13 percent), the Internet (4 percent), and news magazines (1 percent). A look into the crystal ball shows that that will most likely change with time as the youngest adults, age 18 to 24 (11 percent), say that the Internet is their primary news source.

According to *Wirthlin,* when it applies to information about products and services, the mix of sources is more balanced than it is for news, but depends a great deal on the type of product. Magazine articles tend to be the most influential source for somebody shopping for durable goods, whereby in-depth comparison of features is part of the buying process, such as a computer or a new car.

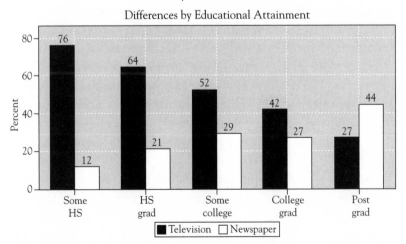

**Primary News Source**

Differences by Educational Attainment

*Source: The Wirthlin Report.*

## The Power of PR

"News Articles Are More Believable than Advertising"

Somewhat disagree
11%

Strongly disagree
5%

Don't know
2%

Strongly agree
28%

Somewhat agree
53%

Source: The Wirthlin Report.

Television advertising has the biggest impact on purchases of less expensive consumables, like cold medications and athletic shoes. Newspaper articles have the biggest influence on purchasing items like appliances, as well as on making investment decisions.

The ultimate common-sense learning is that shoppers are more strongly influenced by sources they consider to be credible.

Relative to advertising, editorial content in the media has much greater credibility. More than eight out of ten surveyed by *Wirthlin* agreed that news articles are more believable than advertising. This is one reason why public-relations efforts (whether health, recipe, or value driven) are such an important part of any communications program.

*Wirthlin*'s survey asked respondents to rate a number of specific sources as to their believability in general when it came to information about products and services. Their results confirm that, broadly speaking, editorial content is more credible than advertising. The following chart divides rather neatly between earned media on the high end and paid media on the low end of the believability scale.

**Distrust of Advertising**

| Most advertisements deliberately stretch the truth about the products they advertise. | | Most advertisements do their best to tell the truth about the products they advertise. | |
|---|---|---|---|
| 18% | 56% | 22% | 4% |
| Feel strongly this way | Feel somewhat this way | Feel somewhat this way | Feel strongly this way |

*Source: The Wirthlin Report.*

Advertising's low credibility relative to other types of messages is not unexpected. People are just naturally resistant to being persuaded.

## Every Shopper Is Unique

Every shopping trip can cause an interaction that influences shopping behaviors, but the shopper's own personality has the most important effect. It is the distinguishing psychological characteristics of a shopper that will produce consistent and lasting responses to a brand and its marketing stimuli. One-to-One Marketing is the terminology and marketing approach developed by Don Peppers and Martha Rodgers in their books and consulting practice, which help companies understand that each shopper is unique as an individual, and that each responds differently as a consumer. There are shoppers who will keep shopping until they are certain that they have found the best price for a particular item, while other shoppers will stop shopping when they believe that they have found a product that meets their needs.

## WHAT KIND OF SHOPPERS DO YOU WANT TO ATTRACT TO YOUR BRAND?

Observe shoppers in the store, or print this quiz and pass it out directly to them. Have them answer each question, then look up the point value to each answer below, and total.

**Quiz**

1. The shopper goes to the same supermarket each week, on the same day, and at approximately the same time, and always prepares a shopping list and uses coupons.

   Circle one:     TRUE     FALSE

2. The shopper never brings a shopping list to the supermarket, always takes samples, and usually buys the product being sampled.

   Circle one:     TRUE     FALSE

3. The shopper always is polite to other shoppers and the supermarket's staff, and will let others go ahead in the checkout line if they appear to be in a hurry.

   Circle one:     TRUE     FALSE

4. When at the checkout and in service departments, the shopper likes to have the staff make eye contact, be helped promptly, and be addressed as "sir," "ma'am," or "miss," and with respect.

   Circle one:     TRUE     FALSE

5. In the grocery aisles, the shopper scans the shelves looking at prices and variety, and makes a decision on which product to buy quickly, almost never reading the back of the package.

   Circle one:     TRUE     FALSE

6. The shopper always tries new products, visits new stores, and always is seeking ways to save money, eat more healthily, and shop in a shorter amount of time.

   Circle one:     TRUE     FALSE

*(Continued)*

7. In the produce department, the shopper will try different or unfamiliar fruits and vegetables, buys magazines with the latest recipes, and always tries the newest and trendiest food products.

   Circle one:   TRUE   FALSE

8. The shopper always buys name-brand items that are heavily advertised, many of which were used in his or her home during childhood.

   Circle one:   TRUE   FALSE

9. The shopper has coupons organized, and instructs the bagger how to pack his or her order.

   Circle one:   TRUE   FALSE

10. The shopper knows the store manager's name, will make special requests, gets easily agitated if the lines are too long or the shopping carts are dirty, will tell other shoppers what items they should buy, and will complain to the store if something is not to his or her liking.

    Circle one:   TRUE   FALSE

**Answer Key**

| | |
|---|---|
| 1. True—1, False—3 | 6. True—3, False—1 |
| 2. True—3, False—1 | 7. True—5, False—1 |
| 3. True—5, False—1 | 8. True—1, False—3 |
| 4. True—1, False—3 | 9. True—1, False—5 |
| 5. True—5, False—1 | 10. True—5, False—1 |

**Scoring**

*10–20 points.*   "The No-Nonsense Shopper"—One of their biggest pet peeves is wasting time, so they will walk into the store with a

*(continued)*

87

*(Continued)*

detailed grocery list, get every item on the list, pay, and get out of the store as quickly as possible. Not ones to act on emotions, they rarely buy what is not on their list, and are not impulse shoppers. They are brand loyal when they find a product that meets their needs. They are the ultimate shoppers, keep tabs on everything, and rarely run out of things at home. Though they do not typically waste money, they will not buy a product simply because it seems to offer a better value. Product dependability, efficiency, and quality are of prime importance. These shoppers are impatient at the checkout and long lines at the deli, and can easily become frustrated and walk out.

*21–30 points.* "The Value-Oriented Shopper"—These shoppers tend to have characteristics of the both the other shopper personalities, and comprise the majority of the shopping population. While they have a need to get tasks done in a timely manner, they are attracted by new concepts, advertising, and will try new products if they are practical. They tend to buy healthier products, and will often compare prices and ingredients to see which product is best suited to their personal and family needs and budget. The number-one concern is value, and they use coupons and compare different supermarkets' weekly fliers. These shoppers are practical and resourceful; however, sometimes they try so hard to rationalize that they become confused about which brand they should buy.

*31–40 points.* "The Touchy-Feely Shopper"—These are the shoppers that supermarkets love to hate. They are conscientious and very aware of feelings of others. They tend to wander the aisles, stopping to examine products that catch their eye. They are health conscious, but also buy certain products because they make them feel good about themselves, regardless of price. They are attracted and intrigued by novelty, and will often try foods that are unknown to them. Their skill, understanding, and creativity allow them to put together fabulous, healthy dishes that are pleasing to the eye. Typically, this shopper will buy a product on impulse and never use it.

Shoppers have multiple motives behind their purchase behaviors. The influences and behaviors I have described earlier are a combination of those that are *manifested* (known and admitted) and *latent* (unknown or reluctant to admit). And, while it is fair to say that different influences can result in the same purchase selection, it is also important to recognize that many of these influences cannot be simply observed in a retail environment and, in getting to know the shopper, there must be a more in-depth analysis.

## The Value of a Lifelong Shopper

Most marketers would agree that being able to form a brand relationship with a 10-year-old has more potential for long-term profits than forming a relationship with an adult. It's simply a numbers game that adds up to a fortune, just like a bank account that yields a 5 percent guaranteed interest every year—the key to success is in the guarantee. The reality is that no brand is ever guaranteed to have a consumer for life, no matter how early the brand relationship starts. Brands have to evolve, reengineer themselves, and always be asking for the sale. Those that do—brands like Coke and Pepsi, Starbucks, Tide, Heinz, and Stouffer's—find themselves with shoppers who use more of their products and pass on the brand's equity to the next generation.

A customer value analysis is important to calculate shoppers of any age. The downside is that the tool is biased against older people. Obviously, the shorter the lifespan, the shorter the period to make profit on a particular consumer. The opportunity is to find those shoppers, regardless of age, who consume above-average quantities of your product during their lifetime. Common math proves that a 50-year-old (with an expected lifetime of 77 years), who drinks three cans a day of a particular brand of soda is more valuable than a 20-year-old who drinks less than one can a month.

Customers for life are great but, reality in the marketplace shows that people switch brands for all kinds of reasons, including boredom. In a 1999 *Parade* magazine survey, taste was the major reason to switch brands for 72 percent of the women surveyed. A realistic customer analysis looks at a period of five to ten years. For example, let's look at the profits that can be generated by one consumer with one product over a seven-year period:

| | |
|---|---|
| Shopper | Betty |
| Product | Frozen dinner |
| Consumption | 14 packages/year |
| Gross Profit | 20 cents/package |
| Marketing Expense | 10 cents/package |

- In year 1, you earn a base profit that remains the same throughout the seven-year period:
  — For example, 20 cents × 14 packages × 7 years = $19.60
- In year 2, you the same base profit as in year one, but two other profit sources begin to develop:
  — Marketing costs attributable to the typical loyal customer begin to decrease which creates added profit margin over time.

For example, let's say you allocate your product's marketing expense of 10 cents/package as follows:

| | |
|---|---|
| Promotion | 3 cents |
| Couponing | 2 cents |
| Advertising | 2 cents |
| Sampling | 2 cents |
| Publicity | 1 cent |

Each year, you are able to decrease each of these categories just 10 percent against your current consumer base, which accounts for 70 percent of your business:

— Your now loyal customer begins to refer others to the brand.

| | | | Year | | | | Incremental |
|---|---|---|---|---|---|---|---|
| | 1 | 2 | 3 | 4 | 5 | 6 | 7 | Savings |
| Promotion | 2.1¢ | 1.89¢ | 1.7¢ | 1.53¢ | 1.38¢ | 1.24¢ | 1.12¢ | 10.96¢ |
| Couponing | 1.4 | 1.26 | 1.13 | 1.02 | 0.92 | 0.83 | 0.74 | 7.30 |
| Advertising | 1.4 | 1.26 | 1.13 | 1.02 | 0.92 | 0.83 | 0.74 | 7.30 |
| Sampling | 1.4 | 1.26 | 1.13 | 1.02 | 0.92 | 0.83 | 0.74 | 7.30 |
| Publicity | 0.7 | 0.63 | 0.57 | 0.51 | 0.46 | 0.41 | 0.37 | 3.65 |

- In year three, in addition to the existing three profit sources already in place, a new profit source takes shape: customer loyalty sustains an increasing willingness to buy at regular price, rather than waiting for a coupon or promotional deal.

You could save 52 percent of your actual budget and use those dollars to acquire new customers! Or, by year seven, if all these trends continue, this shopper could earn you up to $5.11 more than would a new customer.

The Coalition for Brand Equity, an industry group jointly sponsored by the American Association of Advertising Agencies and the Association of National Advertisers report that, as brand loyalty goes up, consumers grow less sensitive to the changes in the brand's price, and that these loyal customers are less likely to be sensitive to competitive promotions, driving down the brand's marketing costs. Dennis Denzel, author of *Managing to Keep the Customer*, says that companies can boost their profits by almost 100 percent by retaining the lifetime loyalty of just 5 percent more of their customers. For automobiles, that means an average revenue of $140,000 during the customers' lifetime and, for supermarkets, the value is about $4,440 per year.

## You Say You Want a Global Brand!

Sure you do. Global branding became the marketing mantra of the 1980s. When marketing food products, however, it is almost

## Billion Dollar Global Brands

| Sales[a] (in billions) | Brand[b] | Segment | Largest Market |
|---|---|---|---|
| Over $15 | Total Coca-Cola (30)<br>Coca-Cola (Regular)[c]<br>Diet Coke/Coca-Cola Light[c] | Carbonated beverages | Europe |
| | Marlboro (25)<br>Marlboro (Regular)[c]<br>Marlboro Lights[c] | Tobacco | Europe |
| $5 to $15 | Total Pepsi (30)<br>Pepsi (Regular)[d]<br>Diet Pepsi/Pepsi Light[d] | Carbonated beverages | North America |
| $3 to $5 | Budweiser (25) | Beer | North America |
| | Campbell's (21) | Soup | North America |
| | Kellogg's (27) | Cereal | North America |
| | Pampers (27) | Diapers | Europe |
| $2 to $3 | Benson & Hedges (21) | Tobacco | Europe |
| | Camel (24) | Tobacco | Europe |
| | Danone (25) | Yogurt | Europe |
| | Fanta (29) | Carbonated beverages | Europe |
| | Friskies (24) | Pet food | North America |
| | Gillette (29) | Blades and razors | North America/Europe |
| | Huggies (25) | Diapers | North America |
| | Nescafe (29) | Coffee | Europe |
| | Sprite (30) | Carbonated beverages | North America |
| | Tide (11) | Laundry detergent | North America |
| | Tropicana (17) | Still beverages | North America |
| | Wrigley's (27) | Chewing gum | Europe |
| $1.5 to $2 | Colgate (29) | Toothpaste | North America |
| | Duracell (28) | Batteries | North America |
| | Heineken (26) | Beer | Europe |
| | Kodak (13) | Consumer films | North America |
| | L&M (18) | Tobacco | Europe |
| | Lay's (22) | Chips and snacks | North America |
| | Pedigree (25) | Pet food | North America/Europe |

*(Continued)*

| Sales[a] (in billions) | Brand[b] | Segment | Largest Market |
|---|---|---|---|
| $1 to $1.5 | Always (22) | Sanitary protection | North America/ Europe |
| | Doritos (20) | Chips and snacks | North America |
| | Energizer (28) | Batteries | North America |
| | Gatorade (22) | Sports beverages | North America |
| | Guinness (23) | Beer | Europe |
| | Kinder (28) | Chocolate | Europe |
| | Kleenex (26) | Facial tissue | North America |
| | L'Oreal (27) | Colorants | North America |
| | Maxwell House (19) | Coffee | North America |
| | Minute Maid (16) | Still beverages | North America |
| | Nivea (29) | Moisturizers/cleansers | Europe |
| | Pantene (30) | Shampoo/conditioners | North America |
| | Philadelphia (25) | Cheese | North America |
| | Pringles (30) | Chips and snacks | Europe |
| | Seven-Up/7-Up (30) | Carbonated beverages | North America |
| | Tylenol (9) | OTC pain remedies | North America |
| | Whiskas (24) | Cat food | Europe |

[a] Twelve months ending first quarter, 2001.
[b] Number of countries included, 30 maximum.
[c] Brands are alphabetized within each dollar segment.
[d] Denote sub-brands that independently meet the global billion-dollar mark but are included in the total for the brand.
*Source:* AC Nielsen, October 2001.

impossible to have culturally divergent shoppers worldwide embrace your flavor, ingredients, packaging, color, or taste. These differences demand a more sophisticated network of customized production than most food companies can manage. Some brands have succeeded in becoming a part of a foreign culture. Only 43 consumer product brands ring up annual sales of more than one billion U.S. dollars each and can be considered truly global, according to *Reaching the Billion Dollar Mark—A Review of Today's Global Brands,* a study released in October 2001 by ACNielsen. "Despite a proliferation of brands in the marketplace and a focus by major manufacturers on being more global, there are relatively few global mega brands out there today," said Jane Perrin, ACNielsen managing director of Global Services. ACNielsen looked at over 200 brands from 30 countries and although more than half had a global presence, they didn't have over a billion dollars in total sales.

The category with the most billion-dollar brands was beverages, with 13 brands making the final list. The total Coca-Cola brand was number one among beverages at over $15 billion in sales, with its two subbrands, Coca-Cola and diet Coke, billion dollar brands in their own right. Pepsi Cola and its associated subbrands, Pepsi and Diet Pepsi (including Pepsi Light, Pepsi Max, and Pepsi One), ranked as the number-two beverage (see table on pp. 92–93).

Three snack foods registered over a billion dollars in global sales (Doritos, Lay's, and Pringles) and four tobacco brands had a significant global presence and met the billion-dollar criterion (Benson & Hedges, Camel, L&M, and Marlboro).

CHAPTER

7

# What Do You Do *after* They Buy?

A shopper's satisfaction after purchase is as critical as all the influences that led to the purchases. In every sale, shoppers will feel either satisfied or dissatisfied with their purchases. This is also the instance in which many brands choose to ignore valuable insights.

During every address that I make to industry audiences, I ask for a show of hands to discover how many companies have toll-free numbers by which consumers may register a problem or complaint. In audiences of over one thousand people, I rarely see more than one or two attendees who have not raised their hands. I then ask the people who have called their own toll-free number to register a complaint to raise their hands. In this instance, if I am fortunate, I will observe just one or two hands raised.

How do you know if you are satisfying your consumers if you don't understand how problems are being addressed?

At a recent conference, I met with a colleague who has three teenage daughters. He told me how they exemplify the new actively involved shopper. He is the vice president of a leading worldwide food company and is steeped in consumer marketing on an everyday basis. His oldest daughter, who had been home on vacation from college, expanded his marketing knowledge. She explained how her brand relationships and future purchases were influenced by how the brands handled her complaints.

She is a busy student and does not have time to call a consumer hotline. Instead, she searches out the brand's Web site and contacts the company via e-mail. She felt an alliance with those companies that answered her promptly and in her idiom (personal, hip, cool, and contemporary), and would forgive the company and continue to buy their product. Those companies who sent out prewritten, form-like e-mails led her to feel that they really didn't care about her or her business, and she would not buy their products again.

When a shopper comes home and unpacks groceries, a product's satisfaction is determined in a heartbeat. If a shopper feels that he or she receives more value in the product purchase than the price on the shelf, he will probably be satisfied. If he believes that the product value is less than the price, he will feel dissatisfied. Dissatisfied shoppers are not likely to purchase that brand or product again and are not likely to recommend it to friends, relatives, or acquaintances.

 Value = Price + Quality + Service

A successful sale is one in which both the brand and the shopper win. The price example is easily understood. Shopper postpurchasing perceptions are more complex.

---

*As more time passes after a purchase but before use, shoppers tend to question their purchase and lay blame on the influences of others.*

---

## So, What Exactly Is Consumer Affairs, Anyway?

A key tool for any successful branding effort is to create a feed-back mechanism that is both honest and becomes integrated into the brand's culture. Consumer Affairs departments have evolved to meet those needs for just about every manufacturer and retail establishment.

It is easy to assume that all consumer affairs departments (and, by definition, their staffing) are focused on communicating and listening to consumers. Perhaps it is because of the name of the department or, perhaps, it's because we are too scared to know the truth.

What prompts this discussion is that, when I attended the Food Marketing Institute's Consumer Affairs Conference, I was a bit disap-pointed. Praise and thanks to the 75 or so attendees from supermar-kets and brands across the country. By their presence (and discussion throughout the three-day session), they have shown not only an inter-est in building a deeper understanding of the consumer, but also strengthening their company's commitment.

That this conference did not attract 500 attendees is the source of my disappointment.

Whether your product is a breakfast cereal, car, e-commerce site, music CD, supermarket, or clothing, one of your best resources is your consumer affairs department. Too often, I've found that this de-partment has been created to deal with problem customers, and does not have a real voice in marketing. It is easy to see why that happens.

We hate to be wrong, to hear problems, or to hear the truth. While focus groups do have benefits, think back to the last focus group that you left feeling good. It was probably the one at which most of the par-ticipants liked your ideas, but the consumers that challenge our think-ing are the most valuable.

A few years ago, I spent a day sitting side by side with a consumer affairs associate at Procter & Gamble. I heard every call and every re-sponse. These calls included the customers who called just to get a coupon, but a vast majority of callers offered insights that could cre-ate new products or improve existing ones. My question is, "Are we listening?"

*(continued)*

97

---

*(Continued)*

The number-one complaint of the supermarket consumer affairs folks I spoke with in Minneapolis was that of having too weak a voice in their organizations.

So, at the request of the frustrated consumer affairs professionals everywhere, here are my suggestions to the CEOs, presidents, and all stakeholders of the brand:

1. *Hire right.* Staff consumer affairs departments with professionals who have insight, good listening skills, and can communicate within the company. Allow your consumer affairs professionals to attend conferences to sharpen their marketing and trend skills.

2. *Call, listen, and visit.* At least three times each week, actually listen in on your consumer hotline calls (reports don't suffice), once a week call your competitors' hotlines to see how they respond to problems, and get in the retail environment to see (and feel) what's going on.

3. *Never believe your own PR.* Always question and listen carefully to the complaints: They are your crystal ball. While the compliments may make you feel good, they will create a complacency that you can't afford.

---

For example, finding an unopened jar of a habanero mustard in the cabinet months after purchase will usually cause negative feelings toward both the brand and the store in which it was purchased for wasting the shopper's money. Upon tasting the product, one of two behaviors occurs. If the shopper enjoys the product, the original feelings of discontent with the purchase are erased and replaced by those of satisfaction and enthusiasm. If the shopper does not enjoy the product, a future purchase from the same brand is doubtful, and resentment over wasting money and food is inherent in the brand relationship. If an external influencer recommended the product—

a friend or mention in the newspaper—that source's influence also comes into question and, in the future, may not be considered.

---

*Trader Joe's "brand" isn't about the products; it's about the customer experience. . . . No amount of advertising can create what we want to create with our customers. Advertising can remind people, but it can't create an experience. It's the personal relationship with these people that builds loyalty.*

—Pat St. John, vice president of marketing for Trader Joe's, *Entrepreneur* magazine (September 2001)

---

CHAPTER

8

# Is Your Message Getting Through?

*Cognitive dissonance (cog•ni•tive dis•so•nance), n.
A state of psychological conflict or anxiety resulting
from a contradiction between a person's
simultaneously held beliefs or attitudes.*
—Encarta® World English Dictionary

It is very common for people to experience anxiety after the purchase of a very expensive product, like a car or home, that also requires a long-term commitment. Usually, the car salesperson or realtor, who reassures the shopper that the purchase decision was a good one, displaces this anxiety. Car dealers typically will call a customer a week or so after their purchase to reinforce the shopper's decision, and make them feel happy about their purchase. The brand marketer for canned peas, however, can't be expected to contact every customer to reinforce his or her purchase decision. The rules are different when the purchase price is a dollar, and the profit margin is pennies. However, the canned-pea shopper might still need the same reinforcement to convince herself that in buying that particular brand, she did the right thing. The challenge is how to satisfy that need. In our information-saturated society, it's not always easy to sort out which sources of information have the greatest influence on consumer decision making. Behavioral studies, advertising, publicity, word of mouth, and the Internet all need to balance in an equation that adjusts from product to product and from shopper to shopper.

## The Medium for the Message

A recent survey by Wirthlin Worldwide shows that there is no substitute for a thorough knowledge of your target audience, as well as an understanding of the shopper's media habits, as they relate to a specific product or service category. The bottom line is to provide persuasive information through those sources where consumers are most likely to be looking for it.

---

*It is critical for brand communicators to remember that no single medium will reach all potential shoppers.*

---

Advertising needs to be discussed and analyzed by brand marketers in two separate parts—long term and short term. As a result of in-store scanning data, brands are able to think more short term. Have a promotion or drop a coupon and measurable sales go up. Information Resources, Incorporated (IRI), based in Chicago, analyzed 400 brands over eight years, and found that increasing ad budgets increased loyalty in existing customers more than they attracted new ones. For the average successful brand, IRI found that only 30 percent of a sales increase attributed to new advertising came from new customers—70 percent of it came from the increased loyalty of existing customers.

It appears that the latest trend in marketing and advertising re-volves around animals—cute, talking, emotional, computer-assisted animals. For the moment, let's call this trend *basic animal marketing*.

You know who maximized the power of this trend, don't you? Is there a consumer in America who doesn't miss those Taco Bell tele-vision spots featuring that once famous heart-breaking, lizard-catching Chihuahua?

It's not this new generation of spokesanimals that keeps me watching those commercials, it is the technology. I swear that I have seen the same dog mouth on at least three different dogs (and different breeds) already. The question is, where will this animal marketing take us and will it take us to the store to buy the brands they are pitching?

Remember all the hoopla with Dalmatians when Disney re-leased *101 Dalmatians?* What happened to all those Dalmatians that suddenly became the pet of choice? And what of those Chi-huahuas . . . where did they all go?

Animals and babies (let's not even discuss the proliferation of computer-enhanced spokesbabies!) sell products. Or at least they have historically. Now that we can easily and cheaply get animals and babies to talk, dance, wink, smile, sing, and do just about any-thing an art director can imagine, will they lose their effectiveness? I would suggest that one of the reasons that using spokesanimals has been so effective is that moments of brilliant use of animals in marketing have been rare and special. Today, with technology tak-ing over the movies (*Titanic, Gladiator,* and *Shrek,* for example) and our everyday lives (Microsoft), special effects are common. And overused.

Some spokesanimals, like the Taco Bell Chihuahua, quickly become icons in America. It was good for Taco Bell, but was it good for America? Are we that easily impressed? Are we that needy for role models? Have we decided that our product's differ-entiation and uniqueness is so limited that *advertainment* (enter-tainment as an excuse for advertising) is the only way to get a consumer's attention?

## Yo Quiero Brand Building!

In July 2000, Taco Bell pulled its $200 million account from the award-winning ad agency that created the "yo quiero" campaign, TBWA/Chiat, and announced it would diminish the role of its current spokesdog. This is a good example of great advertising and marketing gone to the dogs—a fine agency being dismissed, and the finger pointed at it as one of the main causes for Tricon's stock drop of 27 percent, and sales down 6 percent. The company CEO was given his walking papers (and blame) as well.

There is little doubt that most of us in marketing were dog-gone jealous that we didn't think of using that Chihuahua with the teary eyes. He and his potential girlfriend epitomized the desire for love that all men and women feel. He could have been the next relationship expert on Oprah, but instead became an icon that would sell a variety of merchandise, create a demand for the breed, and, oh yeah, sell Taco Bell meals. So, if the formula and advertising were so good, what went wrong?

The first TV spot and concept were right on target. Millions of people stopped what they were doing to watch. Anticipation was high for the spots that would follow. The branding of Taco Bell was strong, and we felt that, with our four-legged friend leading the way, we would have a great eating experience. Perhaps because it's a bit difficult to maintain that high a level using a spokesdog, the spots became a bit less entertaining, less funny, less surprising, and, in some cases . . . just didn't work. We didn't want him yelling out discount prices, we wanted him to share his insights about life. We didn't want our pets to be like him—*we* wanted to be like him!

Being the star of TV spots is one thing, but there were also the promotions. The plush toy promotion concept was a good one, but the execution of the toy itself could have been better. Yes, it did sort of resemble a Chihuahua, but didn't do justice to our hero. What was forgotten was his emotions and charisma.

Advertising is full of smart, hard-working, creative people, of whom there are many at TBWA/Chiat. So, are consumers and TV

## Taco Bell's "Plug Club" Is Brilliant Marketing

The battleground over consumers' fast-food dollars is a fierce one. In the spring of 2002, the battlefield was tougher than ever as Burger King attempted to push up its buyout price and McDonald's tried to grow its customer count, but Taco Bell just might have the most powerful artillery: the consumer.

We've chided Taco Bell for many years for being off target with its advertising and marketing (did they ever find out who fired that Chihuahua anyway?) but these days an A+ isn't a high enough grade for the basis of their new campaign.

It's not about the products that retail for $1.99 under the Club Chalupa banner or their new "outside the bun" marketing initiative—it's the "Plug Club" that makes this campaign worth its weight in . . . well, tacos. Seriously, it is brilliant guerilla marketing and public relations to the masses; an approach that connects directly with consumers. Even the ones who don't ordinarily go to Taco Bell.

Here's the bottom line: Taco Bell will pay consumers $500 through April 15 when they appear on the news or in a newspaper article where they plug "Club Chalupa." The company suggestions include painting "Club Chalupa" on your chest during a sports event—but for $500 expect the buzz (and branding) not to be limited to chests; it will be *everywhere*.

Word-of-mouth endorsements and guerilla marketing are among the most powerful of the marketing tools . . . and those brands that have harnessed the power of it (brands like Red Bull and Absolut vodka) have created a unique relationship with their customers.

Supermarkets must learn to expand their marketing and do similar outreach marketing. As more food is being sold in more outlets, it's the relationship that a retailer has with its customers that will keep their business strong. Typically retailers focus their efforts on pricing, customer service, store brands, clean facilities . . . but rarely do they think about how they can get real people talking about the "brand."

*(continued)*

105

*(Continued)*

About 15 years ago, Wakefern sponsored a program called "The ShopRite Kids in the Kitchen Recipe Contest." In addition to the typical recipe contest regalia, each region held a run-off in a shopping mall. As parents and their children brought their cooked creations to be judged, a four-hour event took place on a nearby stage. When asked, "What's your favorite supermarket?" hundreds of consumers of all ages shouted at the top of their lungs "ShopRite" with the hopes of catching a stuffed bear named Scrunchy that was thrown into the audience. Building brands and relationships are best when done through a positive personal interchange.

Taco Bell's latest campaign should be a reminder to us all to get back to some basics. Andy Warhol was right—each of us wants that 15 minutes of fame. For the brand that can connect that innermost emotion (and need) to their brand—success is a given. All that for just 500 bucks or a stuffed bear!

viewers the only ones that saw the painful demise? I'm sure not. Usually, the first ones to get the message that the advertising isn't working are the ones who create it. Easier said and heard, than to change it.

Fast-food sales have long demonstrated that price advertising works. Whether it is Burger King's two for $2 promo or the string of McDonald's price promotions over the past 10 years or so, excellent advertising (especially in the case of McDonald's) has been replaced by cheaply produced spots that offer price discounts.

Maybe it's time to understand just who buys fast food, and how to influence those customers through advertising.

While the baby-boomer generation made McDonald's and Burger King successful, time has proven that a part of this generation has lost interest in the food, ambiance, or eating experience.

The drive-through window has evolved to represent about half the chains' volume.

Let's break down the current fast-food shoppers:

*The Drive-Through User.*   For customers that use the drive-through, speed and location (including which side of the road the restaurant is located on) are probably the most important factors in selection.

*The Current Users.*   The other half of current customers are divided into parents with kids, kids' after school visits, white-collar early-morning breakfasts, salesmen on budgets, blue-collar workers looking for quantity at a price, people on tight time schedules, consumers who love the taste . . . and at least 20 other shopper segments, each with their own needs and each motivated by a different set of advertising messages.

*The Shoppers.*   Then, there are all those potential consumers, some 50+, some boomers, some Xers, some N generation members and the parents of young kids, who are not going to the fast-food restaurants. That's who the spokesdog was trying to get to come in to Taco Bell to expand the fast-food universe—to increase demand (and the value of the brand) over the long term. It was a good plan that, in this era of quarter-to-quarter measurements, just didn't fit.

Sometimes, we need to look beyond the short term and the budget cut.

One of the most famous quotes about advertising is credited to department store innovator John Wanamaker. A staunch believer in the power of advertising, he was also one of the most cost conscious of marketers, often saying that he knew that, "fifty percent of all the money I spend on advertising is wasted. The problem is I don't know which half."

The tracking and measurements of advertising today are much more advanced than in the days of Wanamaker, in particular the effects of advertising on children. Ninety-nine percent of American households own a television set. It is on more than six hours a day in 50 percent of American homes. Children in the United States spend an average of 21 to 28 hours watching television per week, with advertising accounting for 16 percent of children's television viewing time. Programs can run up to 21 ads per hour and, for many of tomorrow's shoppers, these ads will dictate which brands they buy.

*Raphael worries a lot about his son, Eduardo. He is seven years old and gets good grades in school, but Raphael thinks he is spending too much time watching television, working on his computer, and e-mailing his friends. Because of his long and irregular hours at the restaurant, Raphael tries to spend as much time as he can with his son but often finds their schedules don't coincide. This Friday morning, Eduardo is off from school and Raphael had planned on going into work late in the day, so that the two of them could spend time together. Geri asked if they could also pick up a few things on her shopping list while they were out. As they drove together to the store, Eduardo held the shopping list tightly in his hand. He enjoyed food shopping with his mom, and visiting the grocery store. The managers knew him, and Carol in the bakery always gave him a cookie. As they entered the store together, Eduardo took control of the shopping cart and his dad just followed his lead, amazed that his son seemed to know where every product was located. One item on the list was sold out. It was a particular brand of soup base that his mom always bought. He asked his dad what they should do, and Raphael answered by choosing another brand and placing it in the cart. Eduardo stopped him and said that before they just selected the replacement they needed to compare the ingredients and nutritional information of all the others to make sure they were the same.*

*After they checked all three packages and found the ingredients and nutritional information to be in order, Eduardo proudly announced which one they would buy as a replacement for the one that was out of stock. When his father asked him why he selected that one in particular, he told him that it was the only one he had seen on TV and that meant it was good.*

Advertisers use emotional appeals linking their products with happiness, popularity, and fun to attract would-be shoppers and sell their products. Sometimes, the messages are so powerful that they can have a negative impact on the well-being of shoppers.

The Centers for Disease Control and *Prevention's* Third National Health and Nutrition Examination Survey reported the results of data collected on the activities of over 4,000 children, aged 8 to 16, from 1988 to 1994. The survey reported that children who watched at least four hours of television daily were more likely to be overweight than those who watched less. Their report found that 95 percent of the 10,000 commercials they viewed each year were food or food related. Without doubt, some part of this finding needs to include the fact that virtually all television viewing is done while sedentary, and some children eat while watching.

 **Remember that all consumers, especially children, are vulnerable to marketing. Be fair: appealing to kids may be effective, but your marketing efforts need to balance between what is good for kids and what makes the brand money.**

Kid's snack selection and food requests parallel those products advertised on their favorite shows, which does influence the family purchasing habits, according to both "Television's Influence on Children's Diet and Physical Activity," a report first published in 1989 in the *Developmental and Behavioral Pediatrics Journal* and further detailed by James McNeil, in his 1992 book *Kids as Customers: A Handbook of Marketing to Children.* Overweight kids, as reported in the *International Journal of Obesity* in 1998, are influenced more by the covert messages in food advertisements than average-weight kids.

## Believability of Sources

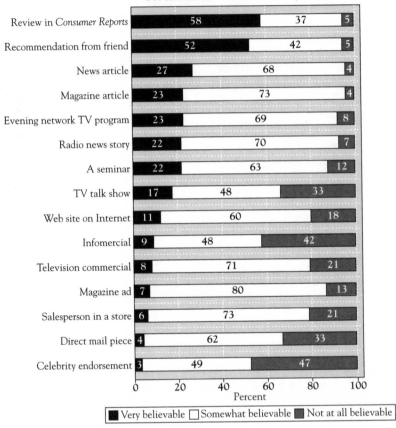

For Information about Products/Services

| | Very believable | Somewhat believable | Not at all believable |
|---|---|---|---|
| Review in *Consumer Reports* | 58 | 37 | 5 |
| Recommendation from friend | 52 | 42 | 5 |
| News article | 27 | 68 | 4 |
| Magazine article | 23 | 73 | 4 |
| Evening network TV program | 23 | 69 | 8 |
| Radio news story | 22 | 70 | 7 |
| A seminar | 22 | 63 | 12 |
| TV talk show | 17 | 48 | 33 |
| Web site on Internet | 11 | 60 | 18 |
| Infomercial | 9 | 48 | 42 |
| Television commercial | 8 | 71 | 21 |
| Magazine ad | 7 | 80 | 13 |
| Salesperson in a store | 6 | 73 | 21 |
| Direct mail piece | 4 | 62 | 33 |
| Celebrity endorsement | 3 | 49 | 47 |

*Source: The Wirthlin Report.*

At the same time that advertising encourages these young shoppers to buy products that may damage their physical health, some groups, like the Center for the New American Dream, feel that the ads themselves erode kids' self-esteem. They catch children in a vicious cycle, encouraging them to eat foods and behave in ways that induce weight gain, while teaching them to see thin as attractive and fat as repulsive, by using thin women and superfit muscular men in advertising and shows. The more a child's self-confidence declines, the more vulnerable he or she may be to messages linking consumption to happiness.

There is also evidence that children increasingly measure self-worth by the products they own. According to a 1999 poll commissioned by the Center for the New American Dream, almost two-thirds of parents worry that their children define their self-worth in terms of possessions, and feel that this problem has worsened. Nevertheless, the same parents have found their kids' entreaties hard to resist: More than half of the parents admitted to buying their child a product that they disapproved of because the child wanted it in order to fit in with his or her friends.

---

*Advertising at its best is making people feel that without their product, you're a loser. Kids are very sensitive to that. If you tell them to buy something, they are resistant. But if you tell them they'll be a dork if they don't, you've got their attention.*
—**Nancy Shalek, former president, Grey Advertising**

---

Madison Avenue faces the biggest credibility hurdle. Only one in four Americans feel that most advertisements do their best to tell the truth about the products they advertise. Three out of four lean toward the opposite view, that most advertisements deliberately stretch the truth about the products they advertise. Fortunately for advertisers, this skepticism is fairly soft. Only 18 percent of those surveyed are strongly distrustful, while the majority (56 percent) only feels "somewhat" this way. Women over age 35 are half as likely (10 percent) to express strong distrust as are younger women (22 percent) and men of all ages (23 percent).

# PART THREE

# BRANDING TO THE SHOPPER

# Forget the 4Ps!

For the past 50 years or so, marketing professors have drilled into their students the importance of *the marketing mix*, or, the 4Ps (product, price, promotion, and place). The theory behind these four elements that had to be the foundation for every marketing plan did little more than to serve as a reminder that each of these must be included for a successful effort. The problem is that too many marketers relied on listing the detail for each P, and didn't spend enough time thinking about the P that was all important—and missing. Obviously, if I had created the Ps, the first one would have represented: *People*. How absurd is it to teach and practice marketing without starting out with identifying and understanding the person you are trying to attract and sell?

---

*Brand marketers today need to force themselves to think beyond static lists and into a more active methodology. My recommendation is to forget the 4Ps, and embrace the 4Fs.*

---

Even if you *were* to add the additional people P with the idea that you could force marketers to memorize the importance of

---

Marketing Basics
The 4 Fs

------------------

Fast
Focused
Flexible
Franchised

---

those responsible for the sales of their products, the marketing mix would not be any more effective.

Marketing today is *fast*. Consumer trends and tastes change in an instant and, as we have discussed, our just-in-time 24-hour media has much to do with the shaping of those trends. The latest medical research report that promotes, for example, lycopene as a preventative for prostate cancer has an immediate effect on the sales of ketchup and spaghetti sauce when reported on television news. Marketers must be *fast* to succeed. The speed of entry into the marketplace, especially in the grocery store, has been cut significantly. Product-development cycles that might have in the past taken 18 months to complete have been cut down to 3 months. The economic pressures of delivering results in the short term, coupled with the advances in technology, have given marketers a new schedule for product development and introduction.

To be the first to market, especially in categories that are fragmented and narrow, may be the only way to prosper and survive. When you see an opportunity and consumer need you must move quickly. Witness the proliferation of food products that are now soy-based, organic, or colored. Heinz, in an effort to jumpstart their ketchup business, introduced EZ-Squirt, a product developed for the children's market that not only comes in a colorful kid-friendly container, but also changed the product color from red to green. Within six months, according to Heinz, their total ketchup sales increased 8 percent. The success of green ketchup led to another variety—purple, which has yet to achieve more than a temporary blip in sales. ConAgra's Parkay margarine has followed the trend introducing a blue-and-pink margarine spread, Parkay Fun Squeeze in November 2001. While it is too early to measure the sales of this product, I would predict that Parkay's Fun Squeeze will have a very limited market (i.e., parents who want their kids to include margarine in their diets, regardless of color or the fact that this spread

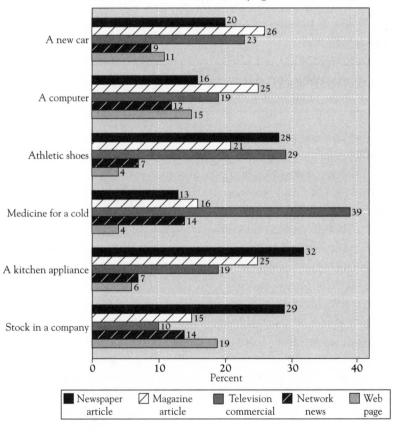

**Sources Vary by Product**

Which Would Influence Your Buying Decision the Most?

*Source: The Wirthlin Report.*

has a lower fat content) and will disappear from the shelves within a year. Bottom line: Find the trend and be the first.

Pick up the *Wall Street Journal* on any given day and you will read about companies that are divesting themselves of noncore assets. Jack Welch, the newly retired CEO of General Electric, who is credited as the greatest CEO and manager of the twentieth century, constantly demanded that his companies rid themselves of products, services, and people that were unprofitable. He instilled a focus in General Electric that forced its reengineering and success. Brands and products should not try to be all things to all shoppers. Your product must be the absolute best in its category—do not divert any energy away from that effort. Your advertising and marketing programs must be focused. Know what your brand is and what it stands for.

---

*Unfocused brand extensions are seducers that will take you off focus, and hurt your brand's relationships with shoppers.*

---

We all make mistakes. One of the biggest hindrances to success is when we hang on to those mistakes. Being flexible is a critical skill. Know when to give up on a brand or product that just isn't going to satisfy shoppers and become successful. It could be external forces that block your path, or ones within your own organization. Flexibility does *not* mean giving up. There are many product ideas that resurfaced years after initial failures to become major categories and brand leaders. During the 1940s, Trommer's Malt Beer marketed itself as "two ways light" (light as you drink it and light after you drink it), hoping to create a market for light beer. In the late 1960s, it was Gablinger's Beer that "filled you up, not out," and tried to get American consumers to embrace the same concept through television ads that showed a tape measure tightening around the brew's orange and brown can creating a thinner waist. It wasn't until Miller Brewing Company introduced Lite in 1975, with typically macho jocks as spokespeople, that consumers decided to embrace the concept of a lighter beer.

Be a brand franchise! Not like McDonald's, but like Nike. Have others carry your brand, and its message. Logos are symbols of how shoppers want to be perceived by others, through the brands on their clothing, jewelry, cell phones, or accessories. Food and beverages have the same power. The right wine or variety of cheese tells holiday guests that their host knows quality and can afford it. The organic chocolate bar that donates some of its profits to charity, shares (and just through its purchase, is able to transfer) its humanitarian and ecological precepts with the person who takes a bite. The coffee bar, which offers a comfortable and soft living room chair to relax in while you are enjoying your coffee, offers a haven from the outside world, where the price of admission is just a cup of coffee with their company logo emblazoned on the side.

Success on the supermarket shelves is not about any one single medium or marketing tool. It's about how you use and balance all of them to meet the needs of the shopper. Understanding those needs is the difficult part—the executionary elements are merely the execution. A thought process too often ignored in the rush to market.

## Store Power

Early in my career, as a food broker working for my father, I learned the power of retail. My father had assigned me the Waldbaum account, and David Karin, the ultimate power in dairy-deli in New York, was the man I had to sell. In those days, most supermarket dairy-deli buyers purchased commodities based on price alone. Karin was the exception. He was a true merchandiser, who forced all his suppliers to merchandise rather than just sell. I also learned quickly that the brand's ultimate presentation to Waldbaum's shoppers was in his control, not mine.

Unfortunately, most brand managers in today's CPG companies have not had to sell their products to merchandisers like David Karin. He taught me to think in the context of the Waldbaum's store environment, in which he tried to get his shoppers to rely less on their previously formed attitudes and more on the in-store cues he could control. The truth is that, even with all the marketing efforts utilized in maintaining a brand's positioning, it is the retailer who can enhance or destroy the brand relationship with the shopper solely through how the product is displayed and presented. At times, a retailer may leverage the display or ad of a high-equity brand to create sales of other brands or store brands. Placing a store's own brand adjacent to the brand most heavily advertised is just one example of this strategy. Some retailers promote their own store brands by giving shoppers a free package of their product when they buy the nationally advertised or leading brand in order to force an at-home comparison.

---

*Bottom line: The only power and control you have is your brand's relationship with the shopper.*

---

## The Power of the Shopping List

The most powerful defense that a shopper of any age has against the marketing influences presented in a supermarket is to have a shopping list prepared before entering the store. Not only will it save money by limiting impulse purchases, but it will also make the shopper feel that he or she is a more prepared, better shopper and doing the best for their family. Good news for them, bad news for you, the brand marketer. The shopping list is your enemy, unless you are able to secure your place on it week after week.

*Forecast* magazine surveyed one thousand high-school home-economics students, and 50 percent said they sometimes used a shopping list; 30 percent said that they always do. Of these groups combined, 45.4 percent said that they were actually in charge of making the list. This underscores the importance of understanding the marketing and behaviors of this generation. What this means to marketers is that tomorrow's consumer is already today's shopper.

How do you get on that shopping list?

The easy, and obvious, answer is through advertising and branding, which can be expensive and take many years. Brands have tried to force their way onto shopping lists by distributing shopping list pads or paying for automatic listings on e-commerce sites. These are all *push* strategies.

My approach is different: Use the *pull* strategy. Create a buzz and perceived value that forces shoppers to *want* your brand on their shopping lists. It is those PR opportunities touched on earlier that may very effectively get you on that shopping list. Obviously there are the traditional methods of including brand names in the recipes you send to food editors and blanketing every newspaper, radio, and television outlet with new product samples and background information in the hope of having your product featured. But what is it that gets the attention of a producer or correspondent?

 **Be the Shopper** Every brand manager wants their story to be told by the press, but less than 5 percent of the PR pitches I get are actually newsworthy or interesting. Make sure that there is a story that a consumer would be interested in before you try to sell it to the press. (And by the way, you don't need to e-mail it, FedEx it, or fax it and then call to see if it was received!)

On average, I receive close to 200 press releases and product samples each week, each one wanting to be promoted. The majority of information we receive winds up discarded within minutes. If you want to attract someone's attention, whether it is a newscaster or a shopper, you had better scream the value of your product quickly. "Why should someone want your product?" should be the mandatory rule for the first sentence in all press materials. If you can't answer that, your product will fail to get publicity and, most likely, sales.

Abbott's Dairy in Philadelphia was, at one time, the leading brand of milk in the greater Philadelphia market. Market share continuously declined and, although their product quality and

---

**QUESTIONS TO ANSWER IN EVERY PRODUCT PR PITCH**

1. Why should a shopper want your product?
2. How is your product different from what is already on the super-market shelves?
3. If your product is promoting a health benefit, which reputable research or medical organizations have proven the finding(s)?
4. What about your product makes it newsworthy? Different from your competitors?
5. Does your brand or product name tie in with the consumer benefit or the product? Is your brand name easy to remember, or will you take more time explaining the name than the product?

---

innovation were first rate, shoppers and retailers were moving away from the brand. It had no personality and no reason to appear on any shopper's list. After all, milk is milk, it's in the back of the store and, according to conventional marketing wisdom, shoppers will always find it.

Milk does appear on most shopping lists, but the brand of milk is usually disregarded, common for categories that have a standard of identity and are commodity based. It's easier not to brand than to brand. Kraft took the commodity of cheese and created a brand. Perdue and Zacky Farms did the same for chicken, as did Omaha for steaks.

Abbott's sales and marketing problems predated the award-winning "Got Milk?" campaign, as well as the growing awareness of calcium deficiencies leading to osteoporosis, by almost 10 years. Declining *per capita* consumption and a relatively boring commodity made it quite a challenge to get this brand on shopping lists but, nevertheless, in my ad agency days, branding milk was one of those assignments that you just couldn't pass up.

My grandfather owned a dairy farm; perhaps it was the image of him and his three sons making sure the families in Belleville, New Jersey started each day with fresh milk that prompted what would be a very effective strategy.

Most families in Philadelphia hadn't seen a milkman delivering milk to doorsteps around the city in at least 30 years. The clean, caring, and kind image of the milkman was an image that remained locked in every would-be shopper's mind. We created an outdoor event in downtown Philadelphia, near the original site of Abbott's Dairy, and advertised an open casting call for a "milkman" to star in the new Abbott's television commercials. A white horse was attached to Abbott's remaining milk buggy, which had been stored in one of the company warehouses. It would serve as the background prop for the screen test to discover the next television pitchman. Abbott's own drivers, now driving 40-foot tractor-trailers instead of the once-traditional 10-foot milk trucks that stopped at every door, lined up on the Philadelphia streets along with over a hundred other wanna-be milkmen.

All three television network affiliates covered the casting call and live screen test, as did both local newspapers. Abbott's now had a *face*—a warm, loving milkman who could be entrusted with our health and happiness. Abbott's brand milk started appearing on shopping lists.

# CHAPTER 10

# Getting Value to Shoppers

*Raphael worked hard, long hours, and Geri respected that. She knew that family businesses were tough and that, in the short term, Raphael would have to prove himself to his father, and would be paid less than if he was doing the same work for a stranger. In time, and with her husband's ideas, she had little doubt that they would be very wealthy. For now, however, budgeting was important, and using coupons was an easy way to save money. She usually reviewed the newspaper ads and inserts on Sunday and found that, in less than 10 minutes, she would be able to find and collect coupons that would save her at least $10. Not bad, she thought, a dollar a minute. When Eduardo turned six, he turned into a supermarket warrior, wanting to buy everything he saw, and making the shopping trip a dreaded nightmare. She decided that she had to somehow keep Eduardo busy in the store, or leave him home; the experience was just too aggravating and tiring.*

*On Sunday afternoon, after church and the family's weekly get-together at her home, Geri called Eduardo over to the kitchen table. She told him that now he was old enough to start learning about money, and could earn an allowance. Eduardo was proud, and felt like a big kid. He started thinking about all the things he would buy with his money. He liked helping his father around the house and to be paid for it would be cool, he thought. Geri had another idea. She explained to him that, each Sunday, it was now his responsibility to take her grocery-shopping list off the refrigerator door and compare it to the coupons that he would find in the newspaper. He would get half of all the money he saved the family. If he could find coupons that totaled $20 that week, his allowance would be $10. If he found none, he would receive no allowance.*

*That Wednesday, Geri and Eduardo went to the supermarket. Eduardo had organized his coupons with the highest values first, to be sure he would get the most allowance he could. As they pushed down the aisles, Eduardo scanned the shelves carefully, looking for the brands pictured on the coupons in his hand. When his mother selected a brand that he did not have a coupon for, he asked her to consider trying one for which he did. Sometimes, she did. Geri couldn't remember the last time their shopping trip was so organized and calm. Eduardo had brought his calculator, and added up his allowance after each selection. The first week, he made $8.20. The second, $11.35. He now averages an allowance of $14 per week, and has expanded his coupon searches to include magazines, rebates, and the Internet.*

## The Coupon Shopper

Each year, the Free-Standing Inserts (FSI) Council releases the latest demographic statistics on coupon users. Typically, data like this goes by with relatively little fanfare—except for those data mongers who live and breathe promotions. However, that is a big mistake for retailers and brands alike who want to get closer to understanding their current—and would-be—shoppers.

By identifying the modern coupon consumers, retailers and marketers will be able to find more innovative ways to appeal to them. Instead of using zip codes to determine different coupon values, the future of coupon targeting may lay within using graphics and creative services differently for generation X than generation Y. As a brand manager, you may not think of it as such, but shoppers perceive free-standing inserts (FSIs) as advertising. They do not draw that fine line between advertising and promotion that we have created (mostly for budgetary purposes). It is time that the brand marketers examine demographic and lifestyle characteristics of the target audiences, then design FSIs (and their own retail circulars) to appeal to that target market.

Between 1995 and 1999, the total number of coupons dropped, as marketers targeted more tightly geographically and demographically. The result? Higher redemption and lower costs. According to NCH NuWorld Marketing in Chicago, 81 percent of Americans use coupons some of the time, with 25 percent using them every time they shop.

In 2000, coupon distribution increased almost 8 percent to 330 billion coupons, reversing the five-year trend. Shoppers entered the new year more anxious about the economy than in recent years. Given the events that started with the Bush-Gore standoff and continued through the attacks on September 11, and our recessionary economy, it is safe to predict that coupon usage will continue to increase for the next few years.

Both men (68.6 percent) and women (85.3 percent) use coupons, however, look in this Sunday's FSIs, and I promise you will see designs that are certainly bland enough for everyone. There is the problem. Brands cannot (and should not) be all things to all consumers. When they try to do that, the page turns and the message and the offer is passed by.

## Newspapers and Supermarkets

At an annual convention of the Newspaper Association of America (NAA), a remarkable thing happened . . . the organizers invited food retailers to tell newspaper publishers about the food business. What a concept!

NAA is smart. They realize that newspapers have lost considerable revenues from food advertising. They also realize that, in many markets, the leading supermarket chain is their number-one advertiser. With the threats to newspaper ad revenues from the Internet, they cannot afford (nor do they want to) lose their food business.

The more than 600-person discussion, led by Jim Lee, then president and chief operating officer of Wild Oats, Al Dobbin of the president's office at Giant Food, and Duane Martin, senior vice president of IGA, set off a loud alarm. All three retailers urged the publishers to get out of their offices and visit the supermarket chains in their market, and not just to rely on their salespeople to pick up the order.

Wild Oats, a month or so before this session, discontinued their frequent-shopper card program. This is a case of a retailer really understanding the lifestage and needs of its customers. Jim Lee used it as an analogy to what newspapers need to do. "Wild Oats advertising must be more than just item and price, our success is built on information and events that are specific to our marketplace."

Duane Martin produced an advertising handbook for IGA's members, which serves as a how-to for cable, radio, and newspaper advertising. He shared his frustrations, which include newspaper sales reps not spending the appropriate time (if any) with independent retailers, who need their papers and reader research the most, as well as the fact that newspapers don't seem to understand that effective food advertising is a mix of media — and that they can't have the whole budget!

Giant Food and the *Washington Post* have a model relationship that most newspapers should strive for; it is a true partnership. Al Dobbin shared with the group how, over the past years, they have worked hand-in-hand to help each other; that a true partnership cannot be one-sided.

*(Continued)*

Don Graham, publisher of the *Washington Post,* agreed. In fact, at one point in the session, he stood up among his peers and explained how Izzy Cohen (the founder of Giant Food) had helped him understand the advertising needs of a supermarket years before. At one of their regular meetings, Cohen had questioned the feel and reader perception of the new poly bag that the *Post* was using for home delivery. He explained how the right thickness of plastic would create a stronger image. In fact, according to Graham, the difference that the supermarket innovator could feel was $^{11}/_{1000}$ of an inch. The *Post* switched back to the heavier bag.

Can we even imagine how exciting (and effective) a supermarket-advertising program could be if we started with a blank page?

Item and price ads have evolved into a profitable revenue source for supermarkets, but are they meeting all the needs of our current and prospective shoppers? What are we doing to educate, inform, merchandise, and excite shoppers into our stores?

No doubt the discussion at NAA enticed newspaper publishers to revisit their approach to and importance of supermarket advertising. The food industry needs to respond as well—both manufacturers and retailers—with an open dialogue and the openmindedness to try more than just item and price. Newspapers have enormous consumer research resources; the question is, are they being used?

# Why Do Shoppers Use Coupons?

According to a recent *Better Homes & Gardens* survey, 88 percent of shoppers use coupons to save money on regularly used products—72 percent of those use them for their regular brand. In years past, brand marketers would wince at the idea of rewarding present consumers but, today, the brand franchise universe is eroding and whatever reinforcement and relationship-building devices are at hand must be used. For the long term, this is not a good or solid brand strategy; it is too expensive and, as discussed earlier, selling at a discount does not build a strong brand relationship with the shopper.

The details of the 2000 Coupon Usage Survey conducted by NCH NuWorld Marketing are:

| Age Group | Percent Who Use Coupons |
| --- | --- |
| 18–24 | 69.7 |
| 25–34 | 78.2 |
| 35–44 | 81.5 |
| 45–54 | 79.0 |
| 55–64 | 80.6 |
| 65+ | 72.0 |

| Annual Income | Percent Who Use Coupons |
| --- | --- |
| < $25,000 | 72.2 |
| $25–50,000 | 78.9 |
| $50–75,000 | 81.7 |
| $75,000+ | 77.6 |

| Employment Status | Percent Who Use Coupons |
| --- | --- |
| Full Time | 76.6 |
| Part Time | 72.7 |
| Retired | 80.2 |
| Not Employed | 79.2 |

| Location | Percent Who Use Coupons |
| --- | --- |
| West Central | 73.8 |
| East Central | 86.5 |
| Mid-Atlantic | 83.6 |
| New England | 83.3 |
| Pacific | 81.0 |
| Southwest | 73.9 |
| Southeast | 81.6 |

## Top Ten Categories of
## Coupon Distribution, 2000

1. Household cleaners
2. Condiments, gravies
3. Frozen prepared foods
4. Medications
5. Paper products
6. Detergents
7. Prepared foods
8. Cereal
9. Personal soap, bath items
10. Wrapping materials

*Source:* Promotion Marketing Association.

It is no surprise that coupons for household cleaners were the most widely distributed in 2000, replacing cereal, the top coupon distributor in 1998, and number two in 1999. Early in 1999, the cereal companies began discontinuing coupons at an alarming rate, believing that they could use the funds elsewhere to build a strong brand loyalty. The result? Cereal sales declined.

Condiment coupons were the next most highly distributed, followed by medications, prepared foods, detergents, frozen foods, personal soap, paper products, and packaged meats. "Many marketers have now realized that a strong couponing strategy reinforced by large-scale distribution is one of the most cost effective ways to directly motivate trial and repeat purchases," said Charles Brown, of NCH/NuWorld and co-chair of Promotion Marketing Association's Coupon Council. "And with 4.5 billion coupons redeemed in 2000, clearly consumers like this strategy as well."

Just as shoppers are not the same, not all coupon distribution methods are the same. In a Mediamark Research Inc. Consumer Study, conducted on behalf of the Newspaper Association of America, they found that more than 80 percent of people who used coupons clipped them from newspapers.

|                    | Shoppers Who Clipped Coupons From | |
| Product Coupon     | Newspapers/FSI | Direct Mail |
| ---                | ---            | ---         |
| Beverages          | 87%            | 51%         |
| Cleaning products  | 89             | 46          |
| Cosmetics          | 89             | 59          |
| Tobacco            | 83             | 55          |
| Toiletry items     | 90             | 48          |

Couponing is far from dead, but the challenge is how make this short-term device that increases sales also expand to enhance the relationship between the brand and shopper.

*The bottom line is that coupons are still valuable and measurable tools that move products in the short term in supermarkets.*

Some shoppers live by them. Most shoppers use them. Brand managers rely on them for that extra boost to make their sales numbers. The opportunity is to bring the medium to the level of the technology, databases, and creativity that has been proven in other advertising and to enhance, rather than distract from, the brand relationship to the shopper. ValuPage.com, the leading online coupon source, is the only site that we endorse on our SupermarketGuru.com Web site. Our consumer panel named ValuPage.com their favorite, because they feel that they can trust the company and the brand. No information besides store location and zip code is required. A quick inquiry on the Internet search engine Google for "grocery coupons" found 130,000 sites in 0.10 seconds. The majority of them either ask for a membership fee or some kind of confidential information, such as a social-security or credit-card number. The couponing medium will never evolve as a brand enhancer if shoppers feel they are being cheated

## THE LOST ART OF COUPONING

What is a coupon? If you ask 10 people today, you will probably get the same answer that you would have 10 years ago. Couponing is a medium that has not evolved. I'm not talking about the evolution of the delivery of coupons (FSIs, magazines, Internet, in store), but the coupon itself.

Coupons should be thought of as advertising, not promotion. We need to put as much care and thought into their message as we do into a 30-second television commercial.

Pick up a magazine ad or an FSI that has a coupon. Typically the coupon is just there—not carrying its advertising weight—just offering cents off. It is the copy and design of the ad that moves us (sometimes) to clip the coupon.

That coupon may stay in a shopper's filebox or drawer for months; however, a coupon's job is to induce trial. It is impossible to calculate the percentage of coupons that are actually clipped versus those redeemed. It would be very interesting to know.

It is great news that more coupons are being distributed, and that more food products are electing to use the medium. However, the key is still in the redemption and moving a shopper to being a brand's consumer.

It was of little surprise to find that magazines' coupon distribution is dramatically on the rise, while most other media (except for Internet coupons) are either flat, declining, or showing moderate gain.

Magazines are targeted and are a backbone media for GenX. GenX also is moving into kitchens, with the cooking skills their boomer parents lack. They are also a generation of casual entertainers that think nothing of having friends over for dinner at a moment's notice. GenX also is well past any prejudice of using coupons as a sign of need. Internet coupons, while all the rage, might well contribute to building the importance of discounts instead of building the brand and its message.

When Coca-Cola issued its first coupon, it was to get people to taste a revolutionary new beverage, and begin the process of building

*(continued)*

(Continued)

a loyal customer base. Look at the FSI or coupon ad now in development. Does it sell your product to the consumer? Does it induce trial?
Or, does it just become a carrier for a discount?

It's well past the time that we give the attention to this medium
that it deserves. Remember the days when supermarket buyers insisted on couponing being a part of a new product launch?

or taken advantage of. As one of our visitors said, "Why would I
ever pay for a coupon I can get for free?"

Many marketers have pronounced couponing a tool steeped in
the past that doesn't have a place in the modern world of marketing,
and have pushed their brand into in-store paperless coupons. Frequent Shopper card programs, with these paperless coupons, have
become a mainstay in many supermarkets. PDI's National Shopper
Lab reports that about 75 percent of U.S. households participate in
these programs. However, the brands have become invisible to the
shopper and those on-shelf price signs are inducing your customers
to switch brands based solely on price.

PDI published a report on an unidentified brand for General
Mills in which they studied purchase behavior of shoppers who
made a trial purchase with a given incentive (such as an FSI or
trade deal). They found that these shoppers tended to make a repeat
purchase using the same incentive. The study found that about two-
thirds of those who will try a new product with a coupon will repeat
with a coupon, if they repeat at all. This finding flies in the face of
those marketers who say that buyers try with a coupon but later
trade up to a full price purchase at repeat.

PDI also found that shoppers who made a trial purchase during
a period in which advertising introduced the product have three
features in common.

1. They tend to use up the product faster, due to the reminder provided by the commercials.

2. They repeat buy at a significantly higher rate than those who make their initial purchase on a trade deal.

3. They also repeat more frequently than trade-deal triers.

For this General Mills brand, the normal brand purchase cycle is 73 days. When television advertising supported the product on air, it dropped to 70 days (reflecting faster product use). Forty-six percent of the shoppers who tried the product during the ad period repeated their purchase, while those who tried the product during a trade deal had only a 33 percent repeat rate. Ad period triers repeat purchased 4.2 times a year, while trade period triers repeated only 1.9 times a year.

# Putting Nature's Gifts to Work

If we were to draw a food timeline since the beginnings of mankind, we would see that over time mankind acquired and consumed foods because of hunger. Plain and simple. There were times, for example in the Roman Empire, that lavish food feasts were common—but reserved for the few people who had money and power. For the masses, it was about hunger and nutrition to maintain their stamina in order to labor. The trend changed somewhere in the early twentieth century as, according to Ben Senauer, professor of applied economics and codirector of the Retail Food Industry Center at the University of Minnesota, food consumers have moved up Maslow's hierarchy of needs pyramid—from satisfying basic physiological needs to a far more complex set of factors.

These behavioral responses, I would suggest, should be categorized into two different categories: approach (think: *go*) and avoidance (think: *stop*). My approach to marketing to consumers postulates that shoppers respond holistically to their environment, as well as to the environment of the product that is attempting to lure them to their brand, and subsequently, become a regular consumer. The environment: color, aroma, taste, lighting, and music all have great impact on what and how a shopper selects a product. How marketers use these tools determine if they attract (*approach*) or repel (*avoid*) a would-be shopper.

Environmental factors that are pleasant, like a well-stocked, fresh-smelling produce department or bakery, attract shoppers and make them feel happy, joyful, and satisfied with their purchase.

**Maslow's Hierarchy of Needs and Food as a Source of Satisfaction**

Self-actualization
Foods to satisfy
self-fulfillment needs

Esteem
Foods to satisfy prestige, superiority
and status needs

Belongingness
Foods to satisfy love, friendship, and
affiliation needs

Safety
Foods to satisfy physical and mental health needs

Physiological
Foods to satisfy hunger and thirst needs

*Source:* Belonax 1997, The Retail Food Industry Center.

Others, that are distasteful, like a smelly, stained trashcan in a fast foodery or music that is too loud in a retail store, or the wrong color packaging can actually repel shoppers and drive them to your competitors.

---

*Observing almost any shopper in a supermarket*
*will illustrate how the basic model of demand for food,*
*and how shoppers went about acquiring those foods*
*(availability, taste, nutrition, cost), has been replaced by*
*a model built and motivated by information, attitudes,*
*perceptions, and other complex psychological factors.*

---

In 1998, Julie Baker and Kirk Wakefield published the results of their study, "Excitement at the Mall: Determinants and Effects on Shopping Response" in the *Journal of Retailing*. They reported that the environmental factors, like design, music, layout, and decor, had a positive relationship to the excitement of shoppers, and how much time they spent in the mall. Other investigations, including that of Sherman, Mathur, and Smith as published in *Psychology and Marketing*, reinforce the importance of the environment reporting that shoppers who have a more pleasant experience in a retail environment spend more money.

---

*Understanding the effects of the senses on shoppers is*
*one thing; knowing how to use them is quite another.*

---

## Food Sundays: Aromas, Memories, the Corn Man, and Consumers

Sunday seems to be a day for food traditions and the emotions they conjure. For some people, it might be about the aroma of freshly brewed coffee. Others might enjoy warm bagels or croissants. For me, as a kid, Sundays always meant a trip to the Lower East Side of

New York to buy the freshest of bagels, bialys, and deli, and the trip to the appetizer store.

This was the store that was the most special and exciting. Katz's Deli was around the corner, and great for a sandwich, but couldn't compare to the appy store, in the mind of an eight-year-old. Truth was, many times I rushed through my sandwich, with the hope that we could get to the appy store faster.

My parents selected from the fish and cheese—and my eyes were glued to the assortment of special candies. Candies that my local candy-store owner, Tony, never even dreamed of selling or probably even tasted. My favorites were the Swedish fish or red licorice laces. Neither came packaged in cellophane bags. They were so fresh, they practically melted in your mouth. The merchant was just that—a great marketer who knew what would attract people and get them to buy. He always gave me a piece or two of candy to taste while I quietly, and anxiously, waited for my parents to shop. His merchandising savvy was always rewarded as I urged, begged, and sometimes annoyed my parents until they would order a quarter pound of candy just for me.

Forty years later, my food Sunday starts with a trip to the Santa Monica Farmer's Market that, luckily, is right around the corner from our home. Stands of organic vegetables, honeys, flowers, and breads, along with a dozen vendors making fresh omelets, crepes, burritos, fresh juices, coffees, and caramel corn creates a fresh food extravaganza. It's our neighborhood's meeting-and-greeting place. Almost everyone has a smile on their face as they juggle the bags hanging from their arms.

Do you remember the old sales-and-marketing lesson about the hot-dog vendor? When faced with competition he raised prices, worked fewer hours, and finally went out of business. No matter how many times you've heard it, it's a lesson worth remembering.

One stand at the farmer's market sells freshly grilled corn, which is a terrific concept. Imagine, hot, fresh corn on the cob that is roasted and mechanically rotated over an open fire. They offer an assortment of add-it-yourself flavorings and spices. It is fun, nutritious, and should have a line around the block, but it doesn't.

I'm one of the few regulars and, each Sunday, I buy an ear of corn. Eating the corn is great fun and is an easy snack as I review the notes for my Sunday radio program. Eating the corn has become a ritual for me, but I'm not sure how much longer the stand will be there.

This grilled-corn-to-go business is a relatively simple operation: put the corn in the roaster, take an ear out when someone orders, pull back the husk, wrap the husk in aluminum foil. Nevertheless, this stand has the most confusion of the 60 or so stands in the market. I've seen people sadly walk away after waiting five minutes to place their orders.

The farmer's market officially opens at eight in the morning. I can smell the aroma from the cooking of the caramel corn stand a little after seven as I watch *Meet the Press.* It's the neighborhood's wake-up call. Most stands are set up by 7:30, and the smart shoppers get there early to select the best produce and avoid the crowds.

Most weeks, the corn roaster isn't ready to sell his corn till 9:15 or so. As you would imagine, competing with a sweet-smelling caramel-corn maker on one side, and a 30-foot-long table of colorful fruits and vegetables on the other is a challenge for any marketer. So, the corn roaster doesn't even try. There is no display of fresh corn piled nearby or samples offered to those who pass by.

Too often, shoppers will stop by the stand and be told that the corn isn't cooked yet. When it is finally ready, the rather simple process that I've already described becomes a Marx Brothers routine, with the two people who work the stand passing the corn (and money) back and forth. The quickest path is a straight line but, for an ear of corn in this stand, the path is more like a curvy road over mountains and through underground tunnels. Too much wasted motion and too little regard for the shopper who is watching has slowed down the acquisition experience.

Here's what happens:

1. You wait your turn to order.

2. You order and stand while worker number one tells worker number two how many ears of corn you want.

3. Worker number two then stops the machine, takes your corn out of the griller, and hands the hot corn to worker number one.

4. Worker number one then pulls the husk back, wipes the corn silk off the corn with a paper towel, and asks you if you want to add any butter or flavorings. If you do, he hands you the corn and you take it to the outside of the stand where there is a table loaded with condiments.

5. After you have added spices and butter, you then hand the corn back to worker number one who then asks you for money, and begins to wrap your corn in wax paper and aluminum foil.

6. Worker number two then takes the corn and breaks off the husk.

7. Worker number two hands the corn back to worker number one who, in the meantime, has taken your money and puts your ear of corn in a bag.

It's a tiring experience without a line, and with four or five customers lined up, the process becomes tense for the workers . . . and, as a result, for the customers.

The price of an ear of corn has steadily risen over the past five months or so. The price started out at $1.50, these days it's up to $2.25, which, although I thoroughly enjoy the corn, makes me question the value of this food experience.

How much value can be added to a product? Take a look at the "added value" of coffee:

At harvest, coffee sells for 40 cents a pound.

At the futures market, coffee sells for $1 a pound.

In the supermarket, coffee sells for $9 a pound.

At a convenience store (like 7–11), coffee sells for $49 a pound (prepared as a beverage).

At Starbucks, coffee sells for as much as $225 a pound (prepared as various beverages).

Food ideas and concepts are easy to create—its still the execution that matters. Sometimes we lose sight of what I'll call the *checkout experience.* Not just the exchange of money for product, but the presentation and acceptance of the total food experience. If you are going to satisfy shoppers, you have to look at how difficult you might be making it for shoppers to shop a supermarket, buy your products, or even buy a single ear of corn.

 **Being the shopper means you must put yourself directly into the supermarket, absorb every subtle aspect of the environment with your senses, and ensure that the environment has maximized the potential for satisfaction.**

It's not enough to be concerned about the products on the shelves. A store might carry the best products in the world but, if the store is not enjoyable, shoppers aren't going to be there.

An environment that meets the shopper's product needs and also meets the shopper's emotional needs is the model for success. Farmer's markets around the country have grown to be a formidable produce competitor to traditional supermarkets, as they satisfy those emotional and ethereal needs. Brand managers should be visiting all kinds of traditional and nontraditional retail environments to observe not only how foods are displayed and merchandised but, more important, to observe how shoppers react to the personal relationship with the sales clerk (the farmer, in this case) and their products.

One of the best and most effective merchandising tools is food itself.

*According to Lynn, his wife, Tom could be categorized as a typical male shopper, who buys all the wrong things when she sends him to the supermarket. Tom loves going grocery shopping. A marketer himself, he appreciates all the great packaging and in-store promotion and advertising that is trying to get him to buy. And buy he does. Forget about what's on Lynn's list, if it looks*

---

### SAMPLING PROGRAM DOES GOOD

The Giving Back Pak, a sampling program, appealing to children aged 12 and under, has raised more than $500,000 for Easter Seals. The colorful six-by-five-inch box contained treats and more than $50 worth of coupons for a variety of grocery and household products.

Sold through Safeway stores for $1.99, the program was promoted through local newspaper ads and TV spots as well as in a full-page cover in a U.S. Today insert, and a full-page inside-cover ad in the Safeway Select in-store circular.

"All proceeds from the Giving Back Pak are donated to Easter Seals to help change the lives of children and adults with disabilities," said Debbie Usery, president of Select Marketing Group in Phoenix that created the program. "The brand names of the products inside are also on the packaging, earning the appreciation of parents and contributing to consumer loyalty."

Dana Doron, a product manager with Sunsweet, believes the program was rewarding for several reasons, "It was for a good cause, and reached the young families that we target." Sunsweet participated in the program by including a sample of Fruitlings in each Giving Back Pak. Other participating manufacturers included Trolli, Procter and Gamble, Nestle, Kellogg, Motts, and Gladware.

The Giving Back Pak was packed through Easter Seals work centers. The Easter Seals work centers employ handicapped and disabled adults. In excess of $100,000 was paid to the work centers for packing the program.

*good, it winds up in his cart, especially if there is a sample of new product. He enjoys talking to the demonstrator, and finding out about the product he is about to taste. However, one thing always drives him crazy—the demonstrator who knows nothing about the product and couldn't care less about answering his questions. In fact, in those circumstances, he refuses to buy the product even if he likes it.*

If we look at the phenomenal growth and success of warehouse or club stores selling foodstuffs, they all have one element in common, not price, but sampling. Instead of just having one or two samplings over a weekend, these stores create an event by sampling six to ten products, seven days per week. According to Promotion Decisions, a Cincinnati-based research firm, sampling can yield a sales lift of over 300 percent during the sampling period. More important is their finding that sampling brings new customers into the sampled brand's franchise. Building a model on their calculations, if 75 units are sold on a sampling day, there will be 30 repeat buyers based on their historical data assuming a 40 percent repeat purchase. If,

| SAMPLING 101 | |
|---|---:|
| Cost of demonstrator and samples | $150/day |
| Return on investment calculation | |
| Units sold per week before sampling | 50 |
| Units sold during week of sampling | 150 |
| Incremental sales: 1 week | 100 |
| Repeat purchases by new customers (40%) | 60 |
| Incremental volume/year (frequency 3 times) | 180 |
| **Additional volume created by sampling/year** | **280** |
| **Average units sold per week after sampling** | **55.4 (+10.8%)** |

for example, the frequency of purchase is three times per year, each new customer will make two additional purchases, and 60 additional units will be sold over the year. Multiply that times the number of times the product is sampled in that store during the 12-month period, then times the number of stores and it's easy to understand the long-term value of sampling.

Too often, marketers calculate the cost of sampling on a per-diem rate and dismiss the tool as too expensive. Looking at just the annual return on a sampled product gives marketers a much clearer (and more affordable) sales tool. The aromas, tastes, and human interaction between food purveyor and shopper create an environment that is more conducive to having fun and spending more.

# PART FOUR

# SHOPPERS' SENSE-ABILITIES

# CHAPTER 12

# What Your Shopper's Nose Knows

*Living in Florida has its advantages. Tom loves fresh fruit and each morning he starts his day by squeezing fresh oranges to make his own juice. He doesn't have a high-tech juicer, he prefers to cut the orange in half and then twist it on a glass juicer that sits atop a quart glass jug. He bought an electric juicer he saw on an infomercial; it promised more vitamins and a quicker cleanup. What they hadn't said was that the sealed container kept the orange fragrance locked inside. He just loves the way the smell of oranges fills the kitchen. It makes him smile, and puts him in the state of mind to start the day by running on his treadmill. He is glad the electric juicer had a money-back guarantee.*

## It's the Smell and the Taste

Aromas are a highly underutilized marketing opportunity for supermarkets and the brands on their shelves. According to the New York City-based Harvest Consulting Group and their BrandSense Report, our ability to recall scents and odors is much greater than our ability to recall the images that we have seen. Aromatherapy, the practice of using essential oils taken from plants or other sources to modify the state of mind, is a largely untapped resource, though it has gained popularity around the world. One Japanese company awakens workers in the early morning with energizing citrus scents, boosts concentration in the late morning and early afternoon with floral scents, and relieves fatigue in the evening with cedar and cypress. In Germany, movie theatres are experimenting with smells of orange to compel patrons to buy orange soda and other snacks from the candy counter. Some Eastern cultures hold a strong belief in the power of essential oils to bring about spiritual and physical well-being, and even cure some ailments.

---

*Aromas affect shoppers both physiologically*
*and psychologically.*

---

There are ambient scents that do not originate from any particular product, but are present in the environment, and nonambient scents that are specific to one product. The general freshness scent in a produce department is ambient, while the specific fragrance of a strawberry is nonambient.

 The sweet aroma of fresh peaches is sure to increase sales of all kinds of fruits in the produce department, but not all aromas are as pure and delightful. Shoppers will run from a retail environment that has too many conflicting aromas (as in some soap or candle shops) or from those stores that have offensive odors. Err on the side of less.

Might the smell of fresh-baked bread and warm cookies influence a shopper into making a homemade meal they love but seldom fix? Could a shopper be persuaded to buy strawberry shortcake in the bakery if there were a display of fresh and fragrant strawberries nearby? Would the seductive scent of jasmine in the health-and-beauty aisle entice a shopper to purchase a beauty product? Could these pleasing aromas even sweet-talk shoppers into staying in the store just a little bit longer in a haven away from the heartless world outside?

The answer is yes, yes, yes, and yes.

Everyday scents like these are influencing purchasing decisions. It's important to understand just how our noses developed into such complex organs in order to comprehend the reliability and power of aroma marketing. Because the survival of animals in the wild depends on the acuity of their sense of smell, evolution has fine-tuned our smell receptors. The human olfactory system developed on a primal level to identify foods and sources, spoilage, and other dangers, but it didn't stop there. Our sense of smell is directly linked to the *emotional*, or limbic, system of the brain, which controls physiological and emotional responses, including pleasure, anger, and appetite. When we smell an aroma, our memory and emotions are jogged. For example, the smell of yellow cake and frosting can bring us back to our fifth birthday party. Aromas, especially of food, can conjure up memories of long ago and, depending on whether the person had a

### Aromas to Convey Concepts

| Adventure | Tradition | Nurturing | Sophisticated |
|-----------|-----------|-------------|---------------|
| Salty air | Leather | Vanilla | Wine |
| Sawdust | Wood | Baby powder | Perfume |
| Mud | Tea | Apples | Cigars |
| Fuel | Wool | Cinnamon | Oak |
| Mint | Cedar | Lavender | Scotch |
| Spice | Rose | Cotton | Musk |

*Source:* BrandSense, Harvest Consulting Group.

positive or negative experience when smelling that aroma, the person will either be attracted or repelled by the scent. What does the smell of cream soda or pizza make you think of? How do you feel when you smell pumpkin pie?

Our sense of smell is reportedly 10,000 times more sensitive than our sense of taste. And, it is much more powerful as a marketing tool according to the Olfactory Research Fund (ORF), based in New York City, which created the new science of *aroma-chology*, and promotes and funds ongoing research on the effects of fragrance. This new science, according to ORF is "the scientifically based, interrelationship of clinical, psychological studies and the latest in fragrance technology to transmit through odor on the body and in the environment, a variety of specific feelings—relaxation, exhilaration, sensuality, happiness, and personal fulfillment—directly to the pleasure center of the brain, the seat of our emotions, memory, and creativity."

## Here's What We Know about Smell

While using smell to sell and brand products is still relatively unexplored, there are a few proven findings, according to BrandSense:

- Odor affects people in a variety of ways, from mood to concentration, to memory recall and emotion.
- When olfactory stimulation is effective, this effectiveness depends on a complex interaction of odorant, personality characteristics, and experimental manipulation.
- Memory for odor is markedly resistant to time, easily accessed, and tends to be characterized by a high degree of emotion, clarity, and vividness.

Many airlines now offer passengers in their first and business class compartments a hot towel. While appreciated by most passengers as a convenient way to wash their hands before the meal service, many flight attendants customize the service by squeezing fresh lemons over the towels. The difference in the effect is amazing. A hot moist towel is a cleaning cloth. A fresh citrus fragrance on a hot moist towel presents a respite from a typically stressful experience. The flight attendants I've discussed this procedure with tell me that the little effort of squeezing the lemon can calm (and manage) a cabin full of Type A behavior flyers within minutes.

Retail store marketers that incorporate something as subtle as a particular smell into a store can actually have a little bit more control over how long a shopper will linger in the aisles, what a shopper may buy, and even which people will be attracted to a particular store. With the right combination of aromas from the bakery and produce departments, the overstressed, harried shoppers relax as they begin to shop the store. The pleasant memories recalled by the aromas keeps them coming back and spending more.

There are millions of aromas in nature, and fragrance houses have been able to capture just a fraction of them. Here are some scents that are found in foods and supermarkets, with their purported effects:

| | |
|---|---|
| Sweet Basil | Awakens, lifts mood, improves mental clarity and memory. |
| Bay | Relieves nervous exhaustion and melancholy. |
| Sage | Relieves stress, worry, crying, guilt, hostility, panic. |
| Clove | Has aphrodisiac qualities; relieves fatigue. |
| Ginger | Relieves confusion, loneliness, anxiety. |
| Grapefruit | Uplifts, energizes, refreshes. |
| Lemon | Balances, refreshes, uplifts; relieves distrust, apathy. |
| Lime | Cheers, uplifts, purifies. |
| Nutmeg | Invigorates the mind; improves self-image; an aphrodisiac. |

| | |
|---|---|
| Sweet Orange | Brightens mood; calms and reduces stress; relieves apathy, worry. |
| Peppermint | Energizes; brightens mood; relieves shock, apathy, helplessness. |
| Tangerine | Soothes and calms nerves; relaxes; heals inner-child issues, emotional trauma. |
| Vanilla | Relieves stress, anxiety; calms. |

There are also many essential oil scents. They are not readily available in the supermarkets, but can be found in aromatherapy boutiques and holistic stores. By choosing certain scents, stores can soothe or invigorate walk-in customers, or the scents can be used in the plastics or with the printing inks in the manufacturing process so that the product itself carries the aroma and influences the shopper:

| Essential Oil | Effect |
|---|---|
| Angelica Root | Creates a feeling of balance; relieves stress, anxiety, fatigue. |
| Bergamot | Relieves anxiety; stress, hopelessness, grief. |
| Calendula | Relieves stress. |
| Cedar | Calms emotions; relieves worry, fear, mental obsession. |
| Chamomile | Eases anxiety, anger, fear, grief. |
| Frankincense and Myrrh | Calms; heals fear, grief, repressed feelings, self-destruction, disconnection. |
| Geranium | Reduces stress, discontentment, heartache. |
| Jasmine | Relieves anxiety, repressed feelings, exhaustion; has aphrodisiac qualities. |
| Juniper Berry | Energizes; relieves exhaustion. |
| Lavender | Balances emotions; relieves stress, burnout, worry, addiction. |

| | |
|---|---|
| Patchouli | Relieves stress, nervous exhaustion, indecision, mood swings, lethargy. |
| Petitgrain | Relieves stress, feelings of betrayal, sadness, disharmony. |
| Rose | Calms, relieves grief, fears of love, jealousy, bitterness; an aphrodisiac. |
| Rosemary | Brightens mood; improves mental clarity, memory; eases pain, burnout. |
| Sandalwood | Uplifts; calms, relieves insecurity, loneliness, nightmares; an aphrodisiac. |
| Vetiver | Uplifts; relieves fear, scattered thoughts, hurt, neurotic behavior. |
| Ylang Ylang | Brightens mood; relieves anger; releases irritability, frustration; an aphrodisiac. |

Great opportunity lies in incorporating aromas into the marketing mix. Scratch-n-sniff stickers on products have persuaded shoppers to buy a certain product, simply because they could essentially try before they bought. As shoppers know, there can be a great discrepancy between how companies believe an ocean mist smells, and how the shopper believes an ocean mist smells. Scratch-n-sniff stickers or aroma-infused plastics eliminate guessing, and ease the shopper's anxiety about buying an unfamiliar product. Marketing by scent is not foolproof. Scents that are inconsistent with the product tend to have a negative impact on sales, and could damage your brand equity. Imagine the reaction from shoppers and their children if a box of breakfast cereal smelled like sandalwood or pine. Aside from the scent itself, the combination of the scent's quality (how pleasant it is), purity (how natural it smells), how arousing it is (the likelihood of a physiological response), and its intensity (how strong or weak it is), all need to be balanced perfectly to maximize the effect to a particular shopper group. A White 60-year-old man has a different set of sensory needs and perceptions than a Black female teen.

DigiScents, Inc. is a company based in Oakland, California, that promotes itself as the pioneer of "digital scent technology." They have developed biotechnology to enable marketers to use scents to promote their products over the Internet.

The DigiScents solution uses a device called iSmell, a personal scent synthesizer. The iSmell is a speakerlike device that attaches to the serial or USB port of your computer and plugs into a standard electrical outlet. The iSmell emits naturally based vapors into the user's personal space. The device is triggered by user activation (i.e., a mouse click) or a timed (programmed) response. The device works by using small cartridges (like an ink-jet printer) that contain natural, oil-based materials commonly found in cosmetics, foods, and beverages. By manipulating gene sequences, the company has already pinned down some exact scents, including some cheeses, orange, watermelon, grape, and various flowers. Pricing for a consumer iSmell unit hasn't been set, but it's expected to be about $100.

DigiScents is pitching their technology as a means by which brands and online retailers can enrich customers' experiences by scent-enabling their sites. DigiScents technology allows companies to communicate about their food and beverages in all sorts of new ways not limited to sounds, photos, and text now available on the Internet:

- In-store kiosks equipped with iSmell can demonstrate the aromas of packaged foods.
- Scented online catalogs convey delectable flavors.
- Consumers can interact with manufacturers through personalized flavor mixing and product customization.

This technology would certainly be useful on a beauty-product Web site to let users sample perfumes, or a coffee house's site, so that visitors can smell the assortment of freshly brewed coffees for sale in their online store. Other applications for digital-scent technology include scented interactive games, Web sites, e-mail, movies, and

---

Insects have the most highly developed sense of taste. They have taste organs on their feet, antennae, and mouth.

Fish can taste with their fins and tails as well as their mouths.

In general, girls have more taste buds than boys do.

Taste is the weakest of the five senses.

---

music. According to Brian Nelson at DigiScents, the technology will allow users to send scented e-mail, to smell 'n' shop, to watch scented DVDs, and play scented games.

eCandy.com is one of the first food retailers to sign on with DigiScents to scent-enable their Web site. Their strategy is not only to appeal to online consumers (with the hopes of getting them to spend more time and money on the site), but also to work with manufacturers directly to develop new candy. Jim Griffin, president of eCandy, sees iSmell as a marketing tool that can reduce the risk inherent in launching new products and enable his shoppers to have more input during product development. eCandy imagines sending DigiScents samples to customers who eat a lot of candy (at least 30 pounds a year), and to major confectionary resellers long before a candy is fully developed.

*Denise was a fabulous cook. When her sons were growing up and living at home, she made dinner every night. She enjoyed cooking and having the entire house full of terrific cooking smells. She even learned how to bake her own bread, more for the aroma than for the bread itself. She had noticed that, in the past few years, her sense of smell wasn't as keen as it had been. Often, she put on too much perfume, so she switched to a spray bottle that would measure out just the right amount. She also was starting to notice that foods didn't taste the same. In fact, just last week, she had been disappointed by her favorite brand of salsa. She always bought the spicy variety, but the last jar was just too bland. She thought*

*perhaps someone in the plant had made a mistake. On her next
shopping trip, just to be sure, she would buy the extra-hot variety.
If that jar was bland, she would call the company to complain or
even switch brands. Don't they know salsa is supposed to be hot?*

## You Can't Separate Smell and Taste

One of the biggest challenges in marketing the taste profile of a
product has to do with the fact that a shopper's sense of smell
changes. You may have noticed yourself how some foods don't taste
the way they used to. The common reaction (just ask the folks in
your customer-service department) is that most shoppers blame the
brand for changing their formula. Sometimes that is true but, more
often than not, it is the shopper's sense of taste and smell that
has changed.

This natural phenomenon is going to create new problems and
opportunities for food manufacturers as Americans age, especially
as the 76 million boomers, who have grown up on sugary and salty
foods, have already started to lose those taste buds.

As babies, we have thousands of taste buds on our tongues and
on the sides and roof of the mouth. It's why babies are very sensitive
to different foods. As we age, the taste buds began to disappear
from the sides and roof of the mouth, leaving taste buds mostly on
the tongue. And, as people age, taste buds become less sensitive.

Contrary to what most people think, it is not the little knobs
dotting the surface of your tongue that are the actual taste buds.
These are called *papillae*, and there are four kinds of them: *fungi-
form* and *filiform* on the front half, *foliate* and *vallate* on the back.
The actual taste buds cluster together in packs of two to 250 within
the papillae.

About 75 percent of what we perceive as taste actually comes
from our sense of smell. Taste buds allow us to perceive only bitter,
salty, sweet, and sour flavors. The odor molecules from food provide
most taste sensation.

> Taste buds recognize four basic kinds of tastes:
> Sweet, salty, sour, and bitter

Each taste bud contains taste cells that represent all four taste sensations. The salty/sweet taste buds are located near the front of the tongue, the sour taste buds line the sides of the tongue, and the bitter taste buds are at the very back of the tongue.

A different kind of sensation, which we wrongly perceive as taste, comes from very hot or spicy foods like wasabi, chili peppers, the gingerols in ginger, piperin in black pepper, and the various isothiocyanates in onions, mustard, radishes, and horseradish. These do not have an effect on the five types of tastes; rather, the kick or sensation is a function of how much pain it inflicts on nerve fibers in your mouth. Also located in the tongue's papillae, these pain fibers are actually wrapped around the taste buds. We consider them hot because they stimulate only a subset of the pain fibers in your mouth, not all of them.

If you ever noticed how food tastes differently when you have a cold or stuffy nose, it is because the mucus in your nasal passages has become too thick. The air and odor molecules cannot reach your olfactory receptor cells, and no messages are sent to the brain.

The average person can discriminate 4,000 to 10,000 different odor molecules. We know that age takes a much greater toll on smell than on taste. Scientists have found that the sense of smell begins to decrease after age 60. Women, at all ages, generally have a much better sense of smell than men of the same age.

As shoppers become adults, their sense of taste remains at roughly the same level, although taste buds do get abuse: smoking or scalding the tongue with hot liquids can dull them.

It is true that some people are born with poor senses of taste or smell, but most develop the less-than-ideal senses after an injury or illness. Loss of the sense of smell can result from polyps in the nasal cavities, sinus infections, hormonal disturbances, or dental problems. Loss of smell and taste also can be caused by exposure to certain chemicals, such as insecticides, pesticides, and some medicines.

Scientists tell us that, as we get older, the olfactory bulb in the brain that is responsible for processing smell becomes smaller. In addition, the patch of receptors in our nose that sends information to the brain begins to thin and spread out—and may become less effective at capturing scents. Getting older means that smells become more blunt and difficult to distinguish. As a result, your shopper's ability to taste food diminishes. As I said earlier, we are really only able to distinguish four tastes—salty, sweet, sour, and bitter. The sense of smell enhances taste, and provides those thousands of nuances that help us identify a flavor. As these senses diminish, food tastes blander. Medical professionals remind us that some common illnesses, such as allergies and nasal infections as well as other diseases, can affect taste.

**Be the Shopper** It's critical to make sure that in new product development trials, samples of foods be tasted by shoppers of different ages, including some shoppers who may have allergies or colds, to ensure you get an accurate and real-life read of your product.

CHAPTER

13

# What Your Shopper's Eyes See

*Melissa's friends give her a hard time about her wardrobe. All her clothing—skirts, suits, blouses, even her jeans and T-shirts, are either black or red. She likes the way she looks in those colors and, as an attorney, she feels that both are professional and power colors. At work, she doesn't wear any makeup except red lipstick and a little eyeliner. Whenever she has tried on other colors, she feels they make her looked washed out. When she and David, her husband, started to decorate their home, she found that by adding certain colors to rooms like the kitchen, she could change the entire atmosphere. She had originally painted the walls yellow with the idea that it would make the room "sunnier," but found that it felt too cavernous, and that the color was a bit too bright first thing in the morning. She repainted the walls a burnt orange and decorated the kitchen in a Southwestern theme. It was her favorite room. It felt friendly and warm.*

## It's the Color!

Product packaging is the most important point-of-sale merchandising tool; the colors used on the package will determine which shoppers are attracted to, and which are repelled by, that product. As I said in the first pages of this book, the average package on the supermarket shelf has only about one-twenty-sixth of a second to attract attention. After that, the design, color, words, and the product itself have to interest a shopper long enough to put it in his or her cart and take it home. With almost 40,000 different packages on the shelves, products need to get noticed, or else they quickly become another casualty in the fickle arena of the supermarket.

*Brand marketers are wising up, and are spending time and money to update their package designs, knowing that appealing to the consumer's emotions is almost as important as appealing to the consumer's palate in getting him or her to buy the item.*

How many times have you (even with all your experience as a marketer) bought or almost bought a product simply because you liked the packaging?

In 1976, I began my graduate studies in package design at Pratt Institute. What prompted this particular field of study was a rather frustrating conversation with a satisfied client for whom I had just designed a brochure, which prompted me to delve deeper into this narrow focus of marketing and design. Looking for additional work, I suggested that I redesign his packaging, which looked like most other frozen-food packages at the time: white background, red letters, and a plain photo showing his cooked product on a plate. He told me he didn't need to pay anyone to design his packaging because the company he purchased his cartons from did the design for free. And it looked it. I scanned the shelves and quickly noticed that many products, especially canned vegetables and frozen foods, had the same product photo and similar layout. A further inquiry found that packaging companies typically also had a stock photo library that customers could use without cost.

While cosmetic companies, led by Avon and Revlon, had learned decades before the value of having a unique and beautiful package in order to enhance the image (and price) of their product, food companies in the mid-seventies were just beginning to learn that lesson.

Over the past 25 years, the science of understanding how a shopper responds to a package design has evolved greatly, to the point that a CPG brand manager won't even consider handing over the design of his or her package to anyone less than an award-winning design firm.

Some people pay five times more to have oatmeal in a vintage-looking tin rather than a simple paper container. Some people will only buy milk in plastic jugs instead of opaque paper containers, even though the paper reduces the damage to nutrients from light. Still other shoppers willingly pay a premium of up to 50 percent to buy their milk in glass quart bottles. Packaging cannot just focus on functional aspects or food safety issues anymore. A great deal of the emphasis is directed purely on aesthetics, and that's what makes shoppers select one product over another, similar one.

---

### *Redesigning new packaging for existing products can be risky.*

---

However, if a redesigned product looks too different from before, brands can alienate loyal customers. For example, when Nestle decided to change the package for KitKat candy from a foil wrap to a plastic overwrap package, emotionally attached consumers protested the change, even though the new package would keep the product fresh three times longer.

When companies update their packaging, often a label is added that promises, "New Package, Same Great Taste!" as a way to ease consumer anxiety. The design of packaging conveys dozens of messages, including how a product will taste and its quality. A package gives a brand personality, and that personality will either attract or repel the shopper.

Color is one of the main tools that package designers use to influence our buying decisions. Our reactions to colors are emotional rather than intellectual, which is why understanding of the impact of color on packaging and on shoppers is an important lesson. Books like *The Color Code* by Taylor Hartman, PhD, and *What Color Is Your Personality?* by Carol Ritberger, PhD, have given both designers and brand managers the data to understand the innuendos and subtleties that impact color choices. According to Herb Meyers, one of the nation's leading package designers and founder and former CEO of Gerstman & Meyers, "Considering that about 80 percent of consumer choices are made in store and 60 percent of those are impulse purchases, package colors can play a major role in the success or failure of a product."

 **One in 20 white males are color blind—and you may be confusing them with your packaging or directions. Red-green color blindness is a hereditary genetic disorder (red-green color blindness rarely affects females or nonwhites; total color blindness affects less than one in a thousand of all sexes and races). Few designers or brands ever give the situation any thought. We use red letters on a green background, list instructions telling us to "press the red button," have red warning lights, and most dangerously, we even have color-coded medicines!**

Just as aromas induce certain emotions and primal reactions, so do particular colors—both on product packages as well as on shoppers, who, of course, tend to dress in favored colors. Being able to read a shopper's personality before a store clerk has to answer a question, or a manager has to solve a problem, or a demonstrator has to select a prospect for a sample, can increase the odds for successful brand communication. The colors a store employee or demonstrator wears will evoke certain feelings and represent the store or brand in a positive or negative way. In your advertising, the colors of the background and even spokesperson clothing used in your ads and television commercials will communicate feelings about your brand to the shopper.

There is no question that color has subliminal effects on shopping behavior. In general, the most stimulating (think sales generating) colors are those in the warm range: red, orange, and yellow.

Red packaging (or brand names that are bold and large) makes our hearts beat faster and increases our adrenaline flow. The color communicates power and vitality and stimulates a desire to conquer. Red also conveys a sense of structure, sensibility, practicality, and dependability.

Shoppers who wear or prefer the color red tend to be traditional, rigidly conscientious, have a no-nonsense way about them, and need stability. These people are strict rule followers, not risk takers, and see everything (excuse the phrase) in black and white. These are the power-hungry competitors and, without structure and guidelines, they feel out of control and stressed. They need to be in predictable environments in which everything is under their control. This is the kind of shopper who will be loyal to a brand or product, who will not make many impulse purchases, and who will not appreciate surprises, like products being replaced or moved elsewhere.

When dealing with red shopper types as a store employee, you must give them immediate attention, and fulfill their demands quickly. They tend to be impatient and put off by lackadaisical behavior. Anything that slows down a red in completing a task (including supermarket shopping) will frustrate and anger them. When they want something done, they want it done *now*. They are extremely productive, hard workers, and demand the same from everyone else. When dealing with reds, you must also be sympathetic, because, at their worst, reds feel sorry for themselves and want people to feel sorry for them, because they carry the weight of the world on their shoulders.

Orange is an inspirational color, evoking a sense of happiness and courage. Orange is the color of energy, vitality, and warmth, which is why it is often found on the packages of products that promote vitamins and health, obviously building on its namesake fruit, which is rich in Vitamin C.

People who like and wear orange are friendly and personable types who can relate to everyone. They are selfless social butterflies, always putting the needs of others before their own. Oranges are natural caretakers, devoted to their families and loved ones; they are the peacemakers and defenders of the less fortunate and downtrodden. Their greatest motivation is to improve life for those they care about, and will rarely do anything that does not somehow benefit mankind. Oranges have a strong sense of humanity, and they expect the same from others. If this requirement is not met, oranges will take it personally, and will have no problems communicating this sense of betrayal. Oranges do not naturally take risks, for they must first consider the kind of impact it will have on themselves and their loved ones.

Orange types must always be prepared for anything; this is the kind of shopper whose medicine cabinet is always stocked for any ailment. Oranges tend to be extremely orderly and, when things begin to clutter up, they can become frustrated and depressed. Orange shoppers buy for the family, keeping their home well stocked for any situation. These shoppers are health conscious, both for their benefit and that of their loved ones, so appeal to their physical as well as emotional health and well-being.

Yellow is the most visible of all colors (which is why it is used on road signs) and makes packages (and people) appear larger than they really are. According to a study by Cheskin & Masten, a research firm in Palo Alto, California, it's also the color most associated with food products. When we see yellow, we think of the sun—warmth and happiness and, often, newness. Yellow is also used to convey a cut-rate price image and, if not used properly, can detract from the perceived quality of the product.

People who are drawn to yellow are self-confident. Yellow personalities challenge authority and convention, and strive to do things better. Yellows have a natural ability to lead, are courageous in thinking, and will not compromise what they think is fair and just. They are strategic and analytical planners but, because they keep their plans to themselves, it may appear to others as if they don't know what they are doing. They have a need to be competent and to understand, predict, and explain concept as well as reality. Yellows are overly critical and authoritarian, and demand perfection from themselves and others. Constantly evaluating and analyzing everything logically, yellows have a problem trusting their emotions, though they are covertly emotionally sensitive. Yellows are the planners and organizers, and think of, and prepare for, every possible scenario.

As shoppers, yellows will buy things they need now and the things they'll need in the future. Their pantries are overstocked with things they may need, just in case. Because of their desire to have everything they might ever need (often in large quantities), they can be impulsive shoppers. They justify these impulse buys as preparing for the future. Yellows enjoy intellectual, philosophical, and nonemotional interaction with people, so in an in-store situation, you must stick with the facts, and not be overly personal with them.

Blue implies cleanliness and purity, and induces thoughts of sky and water. Often it conveys feelings of serenity, prestige, confidence, knowledge, and credibility (the next time you have an important meeting, wear blue.)

People who prefer blue are the most creative of all. Blues appreciate beauty and detail, and are highly sensitive to their environment. They take life seriously, and tend to be sensitive to trivial matters. Blues can be moody, and depression is not uncommon to them. They can be self-critical, insecure, perfectionists, and are highly demanding of themselves and others. However, blues are committed and loyal, self-sacrificing and nurturing. They are dependable and predictable, and provide those around them with a

Blue implies cleanliness and purity and, no surprise, induces thoughts of the sky and water. Often, it conveys feelings of serenity, prestige, confidence, knowledge, and credibility.

All that said, take a look around. It seems that the year 2000 was the year of blue. American Express issued a blue Ultimate card, Samsonite's first foray into travel wear was blue, and Jet Blue airways served blue food—blue M&Ms, blueberry muffins.

Advertising and marketing focus on the visual image. Too often audio (and audio quality) are a third thought. And, until recently, a turnaround I credit to those sensational Gap TV ads, color was in the same category.

In countless commercials and print ads (except for fashion) that I have witnessed, colors for props and wardrobe aren't given a moment's thought. An art director might present a variety of colors to the director who then chooses in an instant, without regard for more than surface or personal likes.

Packaging is different. In fact, many products can credit their brand-image success to the colors of their package or product: Zero Halliburton (aluminum), Breyer's Ice Cream (black), Häagen Dazs (white), Sony Vaio (gunmetal), first edition Apple iMac (blue), and most New York art directors (black).

Color is important. It sets the stage for the emotional tie (and future relationship) to a particular object or person. We usually snap judge a stranger or TV/movie character by the colors of their dress: Austin Powers, Tom Wolfe, Boss Hogg, Giorgio Armani, and Don Johnson as Sonny Crockett in *Miami Vice*.

So, what is with this *blue* thing? Trend or nonevent?

### Trend!

Blue is calming and offers a sense of security that many other colors do not. It is a happy color. I do not have the statistics to prove it, but I would guess that most people favor blue. ("Ask Jeeves" could not even tell me ... but I did find a recipe for pork tenderloin when I asked, "What is America's favorite color?")

We have survived Y2K mania and moved into the next century, with consumers positive and feeling good. Expect to see a lot more blue and shades of blue—in cars, clothing, food packaging, and home and office furnishings.

The iMac broke the color barrier in the office and made people feel good. Until then, no one seemed to care to ask, why tan or why gray? People are spending more time at desks and computers and are more stressed and anxious than ever ... why wouldn't we want a big black box on our desk to uplift our spirits and give us energy? Or use that same color that reminds us of the paint used on the walls of grammar and high schools?

One of mass transit's success stories is in Santa Monica, California—where the city's Big Blue Bus line is profitable, has high ridership from all socioeconomic levels, and is financially successful—in a town where mass transportation is at the opposite extreme of its lifestyle.

In the early 1970s, Frank Rizzo was mayor of Philadelphia. His style was reminiscent of an era of force and police control. His limo was a customized black Checker, instead of the normal Cadillac or Lincoln. As some Philadelphians protested the move toward a police state, a consultant was brought in to help the city's police force image. The black-and-white police cars were repainted blue.

Favored colors change. This color trend will, too, but based on a more thoughtful approach. As advertising has gotten more creative, and computers have allowed us more flexibility (like Christopher Reeve appearing to walk during the Super Bowl), we need to give more thought to emotion and feeling.

Successful advertising and marketing builds an emotional tie. There are now McDonald's ads that touch your heart, Jack in the Box and Taco Bell ads that make you laugh, and Burger King ads that

(continued)

*(Continued)*

make you tap your foot. It's Gap ads that make you want to dance. It has been the successful strategies of big budget advertisers and fabulous TV commercial directors like Joe Pitka. Why is emotionality limited to them?

Sometimes, the subtle tools can make the most impact.

But when can using "color" go too far? In our SupermarketGuru .com Consumer Panel Polls, parents are telling us how frustrated they are by food companies using nontraditional colors in foods to attract their children who are confused by the electric blues, pinks, and purples. Our findings indicate that this trend has a very short life—and rather than sort the issue out, both parents and their kids avoid confusion by avoiding these products.

In 2001, Heinz introduced green ketchup that delivered the highest increase in sales in the brand's history. Other companies are trying for the same success with blue and chocolate French fries, cereals that turn milk blue, drinks that change color as you stir them, and blue macaroni and cheese. Heinz is trying to push their success even further with a new promotion of one million bottles of "mystery color ketchup," trying to make collecting ketchup as hip as collecting baseball or Pokémon cards once was.

According to a March 2002 SupermarketGuru.com consumer panel, 80 percent of adults say the major influence on child brand recognition for foods comes from television while 61 percent say it comes from other children. Subsequently, 56 percent of the adult respondents say children influence the brands they buy.

However, parents also said that there is too much food marketing being done directly to kids. In addition, respondents said while the food companies have done a good job of designing these foods to be convenient, both the nutritional content and pricing of these foods needs improvement.

Trend over!

170

sense of security. Blues value propriety in society, valuing moral ethics, structure, and discipline. Blues often view play as a frivolous waste of time, and resent playful personalities for wasting time in unproductive leisure.

The blue consumer is conservative, and won't be wowed by flashy, gaudy packaging, but may be emotionally responsive to artistic, pretty packaging designs. Above all, blues want peace of mind, so products that appeal to a peacefulness and feeling of well-being are appreciated. When blues are feeling depressed they can be impulsive, but in general blues buy products for a purpose. As a store employee, approach blue people with appreciation and care, for blues are intuitive and sensitive to emotional cues.

In the 1960s, the unwritten rule about food packaging was never to use green. The thinking was that the color green implied that the food inside the package was spoiled and moldy. Today, green is used often, and represents nature and health. Shoppers see green and think of trees and fresh meadows. In the early 1970s, packagers of healthy products used the color beige to imply natural, but soon found that the color washed out on the shelves and couldn't be easily seen. Beige was replaced with deep greens.

People who gravitate toward green are the imaginative idea makers. Highly intuitive thinkers, greens have the gift of reading people emotionally, and finding hidden meanings with only brief interaction. They have a finely-tuned sense for interpreting people's feelings and meeting their needs. Greens are highly creative, imaginative, and have the ability to see the complete picture, which make them ideal for creating opportunities and solutions that keep everyone involved happy. Greens trust their emotions so strongly that they sometimes forget to back up their decisions with facts and sometimes are not taken seriously by others.

Greens are always looking for new interests, and need to be constantly entertained with new things and new products. These are the kinds of shoppers who will try new products and switch to different brands. These impulse buyers will zip through the aisles, see something that catches their eye, and throw it in their basket.

They will choose items that appeal to them emotionally, items that speak to their inner feelings and belief systems. They are drawn to the novel and beautiful and to all things natural. Greens will be the organic and healthy buyers who choose foods that make them feel good. In the store, you will want to use a personal approach with these shoppers and make them feel like family.

White makes us feel fresh and light, and is often used on lower-fat and diet-food packaging. It is associated with dairy products (milk) and, hence, implies the ultimate in freshness and purity.

### IT'S GREEN

Although 97 percent of kitchens in the United States contain ketchup, this condiment is often taken for granted. With relatively flat category growth, the marketers at Heinz took a chance and, with it, changed their business. It was an attempt to create excitement, and boost sales and stock price. Heinz, the name synonymous with ketchup, announced in October 2000 their plan to launch EZ Squirt Green Ketchup.

They knew their shopper and user. Children under the age of 13 consume 50 percent more ketchup than people of all other age groups, and this product was designed especially for a younger audience. The EZ Squirt features a bottle created for smaller hands and easier squeezing, and a new nozzle to provide a super-thin stream of ketchup, so kids can personalize their food in "blastin' green."

Youth focus groups indicated that kids want colored ketchup and, though Heinz initially considered blue, they chose green, then added purple as another brand extension. Parents may have more hangups than children concerning the color, but they will appreciate the fact that this product has added vitamin C, making it the first fortified ketchup product.

The EZ Squirt Ketchup sells for 20 cents more than its red counterpart. Both the green and purple taste the same as the red variety, which has remained virtually unchanged since the product's introduction in 1876.

However, as we already discussed, in terms of understanding shoppers based on their age and psychographics, not all cultures react the same way to a specific color. In Germany, white suggests premium quality; in England, white suggests budget quality.

People who are drawn to white are the arbitrators and peacemakers. They tend to be timid, shy, passive, and may cling to others to make their life happen. Whites are nonassertive and always seek to please others in order to receive protection, support, and security. Whites are gentle and kind, and are best friends to all personalities. They are tolerant and accepting of others, and can enjoy a variety of people and experiences. Whites are undemanding of people, and are tolerant of unkind behavior. They simply want peace, and will not retaliate if they feel threatened. Whites are indecisive and uncomfortable about making decisions that may be wrong. Whites are followers, and will avoid leadership and responsibility if they can.

As a consumer, the person who prefers white likes and evokes simplicity. They are attracted to simple packaging that may not necessarily have much personality. They want to promote harmony, and will prefer to buy items that other people want (and already purchase) rather than what they themselves might want. Often, they are so indecisive that they have no idea *what* they want. They would rather have someone else make decisions for them and, typically, they shop with others. Whites are stores' ideal shoppers. Whites are clearly influenced by the power of suggestion, and may even prefer an authoritative employee to help choose products for them because they can't trust their own choices.

Black is always elegant and sophisticated, and manufacturers use this color to imply a sense of class and quality in their products.

People who love black are drawn to luxury. The shopper who prefers black appreciates elegance and sophistication, and may look down on people who do not. Black is not a good clothing choice for customer-service personnel in a supermarket, but perfect for a salesperson at Cartier or Prada. Materialistic blacks value quality and perfectionism, and are never shy about sending imperfect products back whence they came. This shopper will accept nothing less than

## THE HOT COLORS FOR 2004: A LOOK INTO THE CRYSTAL BALL

The Color Marketing Group or CMG (www.colormarketing.org) is an international, not-for-profit association of 1,700 color designers dedicated to enhancing the function, salability, and quality of products through the appropriate application of color. Each year the group issues its forecast of color directions and palettes; this year's forecast is for 2004—and they are predicting that the trends for consumer colors will be based on safety, community, and heritage.

It comes as no surprise that CMG determined that the biggest single impact on color directions in 2004—from appliances to cars to clothes—is the current geopolitical turbulence in the world. Global turmoil, according to the forecast, is driving the consumer to "hive" (a further addition to the already-established trend of cocooning, so-named by Faith Popcorn) wherein people place a high priority on sharing and on bringing family, community, and culture together. Hiving is a return to yesteryear's sense of community, culture, and safety.

So what does that mean in color-talk?

Colors that are lighter, softer, and fresher, reflecting both a sense of fun and community; colors that reflect a coming together to celebrate a renewed innocence as well as tranquil and sophisticated colors. More specifically, the 2004 color palette will continue to be dominated by blue and blue greens with a significant resurgence of feminine reds and the palest tinted whites.

Forecasted colors include:

- Tickle red
- Moondance white
- Hope blue
- Glassy green

"There is a move toward community and safety in the world today and it will be reflected in the consumers' desire for products and colors that reflect a fresh and innocent sense of our heritage," explains Melanie Wood, Director of Communications and a past president of

---

*(Continued)*

CMG. "New value will be placed on objects and color that reflect a diversity of cultures and our pride in our own heritage. All things classic will be revisited and remade with new and unsullied colors."

How marketers use these colors in designing stores and the products on their shelves will be important. Understanding how colors set a shopper's mood is critical and can generate a strong and favorable relationship. While most brands and retailers are hesitant to change their colors with the trends, the change can also easily signal a hip, modern image without actually changing much else.

---

the best, and doesn't care if others perceive him or her as being snobbish. They also don't mind being perceived as snobbish because they believe that most things in this world are not good enough for them. The shopper who prefers black is not emotional, and has a cool, steely way of looking at the world. Because of their unrelenting quest for perfectionism, these shoppers also tend to be pessimistic, are showy, and are drawn to limited edition, haute labels and brands.

---

*Using color and its emotionality to sell product and relate to shoppers may seem to be extraordinary and unnecessary, but the truth is that it does make a huge difference in the way a shopper reacts to a product and a store.*

---

In a supermarket with a full-service wine department, a clerk dressed in black will not only present the department as a more knowledgeable resource, but may also increase profits by selling up, and increasing the average per unit sales price. Although shoppers who dress in and prefer black value quality, they are even more influenced and driven by status and, if a product indicates high status,

## THE VALUE OF BEING IN-STORE

There is no question in my mind that a significant part of every marketer's time needs to be spent in a variety of retail stores. Watching customers shop, talking to store employees, and observing the checkout experience are all invaluable.

In early 2001, I had the opportunity to lead a group of retailers and manufacturers on a multistore tour arranged by the International Dairy Deli Bakery Association (IDDBA) in San Antonio and Austin, Texas.

The tour included the favorites: Central Market, HEB, HEB Fresh Store, Fiesta, Randall's, and Albertson's. No question each of the stores had something different to say and to learn from—some more than others, even to this group of highly experienced top-level executives.

Each time I visit a store (and my goal is 15 per week), I learn something new. It could be a new product, new display technique, new retail format, or just a new insight into consumer behavior at retail.

Walking the aisles with the IDDBA group was even better than doing it alone. The group was able to share each other's insights and sightings and build on them.

There is no question in my mind that in this case, a committee can be more useful than an individual, if the committee can leave their egos at the door and communicate effectively. That's just what happened on this trip.

Within a specific company, it is hard to get beyond all the corporate baggage. In an environment set up by a third party, in this case, a leading trade association, people relax more and can be truer to themselves, honest, and sharing.

The role of trade associations must change. Too many rely on revenue from trade shows that, due to both retailer and manufacturer consolidation, is declining. Food associations must offer more formalized store tours for all members of CPG brands. My experience has been that the sales folks readily join in (understanding that some retailers are usually in the group), but seldom do the marketing groups.

*(Continued)*

In fact, I will be so bold as to say that many marketing types go out of their way to avoid store tours. That is a big mistake.

No matter what the product or service, you have got to be a part of the *selling* process to understand consumers. It's not enough to create award-winning ads and marketing programs that win awards. You've got to see, touch, and feel the retail experience.

We have some of the most important marketing tools at our fingertips. Too often, they are ignored. Visiting stores is a *must* in every marketing mix, and it's the marketing folks at the top (as well as the bottom) that need to get into the stores to see what is happening.

that's what they'll buy. In the store, remember that these people want to impress, so present to them elite, top-shelf products with as much grandeur as you can muster. A sample piece of cheddar cheese needs to be presented as if it were Beluga. Emphasize to them how exclusive the product is, and it's as good as sold.

While a great package design can draw a shopper's attention, the product still has to stand on its own.

 **Be the Shopper**

**Taste is still number one! Shoppers want foods that taste great. Health is important, as is convenience and price, but unless it tastes great, you have little more than a commodity that can be easily replaced.**

Knowing and using color triggers and emotions will help you turn the marketing and merchandising odds in your favor. The test I always use to determine just how much impact a package will have is to place the package on the shelf in the store in the location in which it will actually appear. I then walk fifteen feet away, and see if it attracts my attention. If the brand name is clearly visible, and if any of the major call to action words (such as organic, new flavor, or supersize) are readable.

CHAPTER

14

# Lights, Music . . . Action

Before moving to Boston, Chris and Kim had lived in Minneapolis. While they liked the supermarket they now frequented, they missed the Byerly's at which Kim's family had always shopped. Not only was there great service and every product you could imagine, but the store felt good. Most of the floor was carpeted, and there was a huge crystal chandelier in the front of the store. The chandelier was a bit gauche for their taste, but the warm light it cast in the store made it feel more like a home than a supermarket. When Chris and Kim moved, they visited a half-dozen or so supermarkets before deciding which one they would frequent. They chose a Super Stop & Shop, which was filled with light. Chris hated a dirty food store. He had worked in a large deli the summer between his sophomore and junior years in college, and became an amateur food inspector. He always looked in the corners of the meat and deli cases to see if they were spotless and hated those stores that lowered their lights to set a mood for the department. He told Kim that he wanted to see what he was *buying. Kim, on the other hand, cared more about the overall ambience of the store. She missed the carpeting of Byerly's, but the soft music that this store played made up for it. She always looked forward to holiday time. Starting a week before Thanksgiving and continuing through New Year's Day, this store always brought in a grand piano and had a series of pianists playing holiday music nonstop. The music made her think back to those fabulous holiday meals that her grandmother made.*

## Natural Light Makes a Difference

Pacific Gas & Electric, the power utility, commissioned the Heschong Mahone Group, based in Fair Oaks, California, to determine if daylight in a retail environment had an effect on sales. The study focused on the sales performance of a chain retailer who operates 108 nearly identical stores. Two-thirds of the stores have skylighting (allowing the sun's natural rays to enter the store), and one third do not. The electric lighting in all stores was primarily fluorescent.

The study found that the skylights often provided far more illumination, often two to three times the target illumination levels. Photo-sensor controls turned off some of the fluorescent lights when daylight levels exceeded target illumination.

The monthly gross sales per store were averaged over an 18-month period that went from February 1 to August 31 of the following year. This average sales figure was transformed into a *sales index*, which was statistically reliable, but that did not reveal actual dollar performance.

 Is lighting always good? I suggest you always remember the environment. At a grand opening of a supermarket in Florida, the store manager proudly remarked to me how the entranceway was so beautiful that his new customers would actually stop in their tracks as they entered in order to take in the store's beauty. Actually, the glare from the sun was hurting many customers' eyes as they entered the store and that's why they were stopping. The manager was surprised and a bit embarrassed to see that once the glare spot was covered with a floor mat his customers didn't even hesitate to begin their shopping.

The skylights were found to be positively and significantly correlated to higher sales. All other things being equal, an average nonskylit store in the chain would be likely to increase its sales by 40 percent with the addition of skylights, with a probable range somewhere between 31 percent and 49 percent. The PG&E study reports this finding with 99 percent statistical certainty.

The presence of skylights was the best predictor of the sales per store of all the controlled variables considered, after the number of hours open per week. If a typical nonskylit store were averaging sales of $2 per square foot, the findings show that the store's sales might be expected to increase to somewhere between $2.61 to $2.98 per square foot with the addition of a skylighting system.

The skylights have had a major impact on the overall operation of the chain. Heschong Mahone Group suggests that, based on this study, if the chain was to add the skylighting system to the remaining third of their stores, their yearly gross sales would increase by 11 percent. The difference between having none of their stores skylit, and all their stores skylit is a 40 percent increase in gross sales for the retail chain.

## Rolling Stones or Sinatra? Destiny's Child or Dwight Yoakam?

*Music is a powerful marketing tool. It spans all generations, and can segment would-be buyers with just a few notes of a particular tune.*

Brand advertising uses the power of music on television and radio; retailers use their PA systems to influence how long people stay in stores and what they buy. Music is capable of evoking a smile, a scream, a kiss, or anger. Its impact on consumer behavior in the supermarket is now readily acknowledged, and is used in the mainstream, as companies like Muzak have perfected which songs to play at which time of the day. A Barry Manilow love song played midday may well seduce a housewife into making a roman-tic candlelit dinner for her husband, while fast-paced songs get the lines moving and people out of the store faster on Saturday morning.

The familiar sounds that our ears pick up are memorable and easily transferred to the shopping activity and brand selections that are taking place. A Beatles song, known long ago by a baby boomer, and stuck in his or her memory, brings up memories of youth and simplicity. The tune now used in a commercial for a brand surely increases its success of trial because of the affinity. The basics of music are volume, pitch, tempo, and rhythm. However, it is the de-gree to which a shopper likes the music, its emotionality, that can evoke the strongest reaction and strengthen the relationship be-tween brand and shopper. According to Complete Audio GmbH, a Hamburg, Germany–based music-consultancy firm, music stimu-lates a shopper's readiness to absorb information as well as creating the necessary preconditions for a successful advertisement. Their studies show that music played in a minor key gives rise to a sense of melancholy, sadness, or mystery. Major keys and fast tempos pro-voke positive and uplifting emotions.

Ronald Millman conducted studies that used background music to affect behavior in supermarket and restaurant settings. His find-ings were published in the *Journal of Consumer Research*, and proved that in-store supermarket traffic flow could be controlled by tempo. He also found that in the restaurant setting slower music had the ef-fect of patrons taking more time to eat their meals and increasing revenue of alcoholic beverages.

Too loud or too soft? You can never have it right for everyone. Adjust the volume to the tastes of the majority of your shoppers. And remember that many aging boomers are beginning to wear hearing aids; a little too much Zeppelin under the headphones has begun to take its toll. Excellent customer service means listening, and when customers complain about the sound or tonality of the music, respond quickly, otherwise they will leave and shop elsewhere.

In 1988, Richard Yalch and Eric Spangenberg published their study, "An Environmental Psychological Study of Foreground and Background Music as Retail Atmospheric Factors" in the *AMA Educators' Conference Proceedings*, which built on Millman's initial research. The study compared the effects of foreground music (Top 40), and background music (instrumental easy listening), to a no-music control group in a department store. The under-25-year-olds reported that they had spent more time shopping in the easy-listening environment, whereas older shoppers perceived that they had shopped longer when Top 40 music was being played. Another survey, conducted by Drs. Leigh McAlister and Michael Rothschild and reported in *Advances in Consumer Research*, found that playing classical music in a wine cellar resulted in customers buying more expensive wine than when Top 40 music was played.

Music can also be used as a promotional tool. Starbuck's CD selections sell well, and remind shoppers that the Starbucks experience is about lifestyle, not just product. One of the most unlikely and successful music and food promotions is a partnership between Wendy's and *Rolling Stone* magazine.

Feeling that music and hamburgers have always been entwined, the third-largest quick-serve hamburger chain created this promotion, now in its second year, to discover an exciting new tune that embodies the characteristics of their signature product. "Wendy's Search for Sizzling Sounds" is a summertime contest partnered with Rollingstone.com. Music reviewers from the site and music experts from TNN/CMT serve as judges for the original entries. Songs must reflect the creators' passion for hot-and-juicy hamburgers and are judged on creativity, originality, lyrics, and melody. Tunes can be in any musical genre, and lyric-only entries are not being accepted.

The grand-prize winner receives a daylong recording session at Marwyn Studios in Nashville, and get the opportunity to meet with top music producers like Wynn Jacks, who produced music for Shania Twain, Garth Brooks, and the Dixie Chicks. Two finalists perform their songs on the Late Late Show with Craig Kilborne, and five runners-up will receive home musical and recording equipment worth $3,000.

It's a smart use of music that goes well beyond just a tune in a 30-second spot. It reaches out to current and would-be shoppers with an emotional message that says you are a part of our family, and we have similar lives—come buy your burgers here.

Retailers use Christmas music to create an environment conducive to buying decorations and gifts. Seasonal in-store events like Food & Wine from France's April in Paris or Oktoberfest become more effective (and profitable) when the event's traditional music is added to the marketing plan.

Music, just like a logo, can help to build a brand relationship and image through recall, and the emotional connection the shopper has with the tune. A familiar tune or even just a string of music can also reduce the anxiety of a new shopper who is unfamiliar with the brand or product by building confidence in the emotional association with the brand. Selecting the music that becomes part of your brand is as important as the selection of your logo and brand name and can be just as difficult. My recommendation as to how to maximize your success in selecting the correct music is to collect input from shoppers. If you have a consumer hotline, ask the operators to ask one final question after they have satisfied the caller's request. It's as easy as "What music or song do you think would best represent our brand?"

Just as with all your other marketing and advertising work, you have to separate your own feelings, likes, and dislikes from your creative product. You might be a baby boomer that enjoys Barbra Streisand's music and feel it would be perfect for your brand of frozen easy-to-prepare gourmet dinners only to find that the shoppers you want as customers connect more with the more soulful and hard-driving sound of Tina Turner.

*Roger's father had been the manager of the men's suit department in the same department store at which Roger was now the vice president. In those days, stores grouped all the men's clothing together into one department, instead of today's mini-departments, segmented by designer. His father had been a very successful salesman, always selling more suits than anyone else. His key to success, he had told Roger, was simple. Before he went over to a shopper he would observe how they looked at the suits. If they were looking at the designs or colors he would let another one of the salespeople take care of them. He would look for the shopper that was feeling the fabrics. He knew that these men were ready to buy, and buy more than just one suit. He was always able to sell an extra pair of pants, or sport jacket, or tie to the shopper who "felt first."*

## Maybe It's the Touch?

We have all known people who can be described as touchy-feely. That person hugs, constantly reaches out to make contact with another human being, and is very responsive to kinesthetic stimuli. Touch is a difficult sense to describe as a marketing tool. There is no doubt that a shopper who is comparing two similar products will take into consideration the feel of the product. Perhaps it's weight, the solidity of the package (or, in the case of produce, the texture), the temperature, or how it fits his or her hand, that will make the difference between sale and no sale.

---

### Effects of P-O-P

- A sign communicating a brand message on a display increased sales, per store per week, by +2 percent in one brand and 6 percent in another.

- Addition of base or case wrap to the display increased total sales to +12 percent.

- Adding a standee increased total sales +27 percent.

- An inflatable or mobile increased sales +40 percent.

- Adding a sign that communicated the brand's thematic tie-in with a sport, movie, or charity increased results to +65 percent.

*Source:* Point-of-Purchase Advertising International and Advertising Research Foundation 2001 Supermarket Study.

---

Joann Peck and Terry Childers, in their research study for The Retail Food Industry Center, *Point-of-Purchase Signs, Impulse Purchases, and Individual Differences in the "Desire to Touch,"* attempt to give marketing credibility to the role of touch in a supermarket environment. Their research, based on studying shopper behavior in a supermarket produce department (specifically, at a display of peaches and nectarines), was able to determine that people who measure high in their desire to touch are more likely to approach and touch products and to make impulse purchases. The research also concluded that point-of-purchase signs that encouraged shoppers to touch (with wording like "feel the freshness"), stimulated impulse purchases among shoppers who had high tendencies to touch. Ten percent of the group had reported that until they had been attracted to the display and touched the fruit or seen the sign urging them to feel the fruit, they had not planned to buy any fruit on that day's shopping trip. Twenty-five percent of the shoppers, who had purchased either peaches or nectarines had not planned on buying either of these specific fruits.

## ARE THE DAYS OF CANNED TUNA NUMBERED?

One of the biggest marketing challenges is when a package's shape or materials change.

Since its inception, in around 1903, canned tuna fish has been as much a part of America as apple pie. For supermarket retailers, this little package has become a highly effective tool which, when promoted on sale, is practically a guarantee to bring shoppers into stores. For shoppers, it is a familiar and trusted shape.

Canned tuna has become a pantry staple. Whether it's tuna-salad sandwiches for the kids, tuna-noodle casserole for the family, or simply tuna straight out of the can; this is probably the original convenience food. Canned tuna is America's favorite fish with per-capita consumption at 3.5 lbs, and accounting for 23 percent of all fish and seafood consumption.

Although that might sound like a terrific business, it's important to note that canned tuna is a relatively flat category, with prices declining as consumers expand their taste buds to include other varieties of fish.

StarKist jump-started this category with innovation and value-added products—and our May 2001 SupermarketGuru.com Consumer Panel Report confirms that they did just that.

After spending 98 years selling canned tuna, StarKist introduced tuna in a vacuum-sealed, nonrecyclable, foil-lined pouch that contains less liquid than does the can. For consumers, that means no more can openers and no more drippy messes. StarKist claims that the flavor is fresher than ever. For the company, it might just mean added profits along with creating a strong customer loyalty.

The question is: Will America embrace the new feel of tuna or will the traditional metal can prevail? What effect, if any, will it have on the consumption and price points of tuna?

The SupermarketGuru.com Consumer Panel Report:

- Four thousand, eight hundred and fifty-five consumers completed our online survey, of which 83 percent were women.

- Ninety-four percent currently purchase canned tuna.

*(continued)*

*(Continued)*

- By the end of May 2001, 31 percent of the SupermarketGuru.com Consumer Panel (1,505 shoppers) had already tried the StarKist Tuna in a pouch, which is a significant trial for any new product (yet one in a relatively noninnovative category).

- Seventy-five percent, or three out of four, found it to be more convenient than the canned variety. Less than half (44 percent versus 56 percent) found the taste to be better than canned.

One surprising finding was that, while we all know that dented or bulging cans could indicate presence of the botulism nerve toxin (which could cause paralysis or even death if ingested), only about half of the respondents were concerned at all about the safety of dented cans. Clearly, one more advantage to this type of packaging is food safety.

The bottom line is that StarKist's packaging innovation is a major hit, and could even take the product out of the commodity category and elevate it to near value-added. The challenge will be convincing consumers that tuna in a can should be replaced.

In addition to mass advertising, StarKist's key to success will be in store sampling, couponing, and direct mailing live product samples to people at home.

It's possible that, by the time canned tuna reaches its 100th birthday, the pouch could outsell the can that created the convenience foods industry.

There are two lessons to be learned from this research.

*The first is that whenever possible and appropriate to the product, the wording and photos on point-of-sale and product packaging should be as kinesthetic as would be believable by a shopper.*

The fruit-flavored beverage with a beautiful orchard scene and the slogan "tastes like it was just picked," would without question attract

### The Mien Shiang Marketing Strategy: Reading Faces

#### by Patricia McCarthy

The age-old Taoist practice of *Mien Shiang* is an art and a science that means literally face (*mien*) reading (*shiang*). It is an accurate means of self-discovery, and a great way to help us understand others. As the ancient Taoists said, *the face records the past, reflects the present, and forecasts the future.*

Simply by looking at someone's face, we can determine his or her character, personality, health, wealth potential, social standing, and longevity. And the types of products they are most likely to buy in a supermarket.

What we look for when we read a face are the characteristics associated with the shape of the face as well as the sizes, shapes, and positions of each facial feature. The lines, shadings, and marking that appear over time on the face also reveal much of who we are and who we are likely to become.

#### Our Faces Accurately Record Our Chronological Passages of Life

Certain facial traits are inherited from our parents and our ancestors, while others are acquired. These acquired lines, shadings, and shapes should be celebrated as proof that we have learned our life lessons. If we don't do our life's work at the proper times, we can suffer emotionally, physically, and spiritually. So, it's good to see those markings of passage appear on our faces. People don't value wisdom if they don't value aging.

#### Here's Looking at You

Mien Shiang is not about reading facial expressions. Many people have good poker faces; They are experts at covering up their feelings by controlling their expressions. A good bluffer can easily change a look or a movement to fool others. But shapes, positions, lines, shadows, and other facial markings tell the truth. They are foolproof signs, if you know how to read them.

*(continued)*

189

*(Continued)*

## Finding the Zone

In Mien Shiang, there are three primary zones to separate three personality types.

Look at the people around you. If your eyes are drawn to the top part of one person's face (to the strong, high, broad forehead, distinct hairline) this person has a Mental Zone personality. These people are the thinkers, analyzing and reanalyzing details, weighing pros and cons. An example of a Mental Zone person would be Albert Einstein, a man who spent much of his time in his head. To market to this kind of person, you need to appeal to him or her with details. They are the deliberate and hesitant buyers, and they need to see lists and statistics, what the research says, what the safety record is. They will buy the top-three healthiest foods and the best-rated products on the market.

If the person you're analyzing has strong features in the middle of the face (prominent long nose, high cheekbones, and high eyebrows giving an aloof look) this person has a Practical Zone personality. These people are the most efficient of all, wanting to save time and money. These calculated buyers want everything to make sense, so appeal to their desire for the most and best efforts for their dollars. Middle Zone people want the bargains, but they won't settle for shoddy quality. They want the extra free bagels, but they also must have the best bagels. They will buy healthy food because it makes sense (and cents!) not to lose profitable work time being sick.

If the bottom part of a person's face (full mouth, prominent chin, or fleshy jaw) is the focus, he or she has an Intuitive/Emotional personality. These people act on impulse based on their feelings, not their logic. Intuitive types want to feel good, and will instinctively buy products that appeal to their basic creature comforts. They will buy feel-good products over healthy products because they are more interested in immediate gratification than the long-range health benefits. Appeal to their instinctive wants, not just needs, in product and packaging. Make them say, I want that, I love the packaging, I love this, I love that. These are the people who you may be able to sell to using savvy packaging and marketing alone.

### Beyond the Zones: Wu Xing, the Five Elements

More specifically, in reading the face we use the characteristics associated with Wu Xing (The Five Elements) and each of these element types have characteristics that will be drawn to particular colors, aromas, flavors, and special foods.

A person who has a strong Earth element in their face (square face, full lips, fleshy chin, yellow complexions) tends to favor sweets, and root vegetables, soups, baked pies, and anything considered a nurturing food. They're especially drawn to yellow and brown foods (as in root, of the earth, veggies, etc.) as well as yellow, earthy, and old-fashioned, home-style packaging.

Someone with strong Metal Element facial characteristics (round face, long straight nose, high cheekbones, hollow cheeks, light or high-sheen skin tones) has exquisite taste and pays close attention to detail. Since the Metal Element people often have a highly developed sense of smell, aroma is always a consideration—not just in the food, but in the store itself. They are drawn to cool, light-colored foods that are crisp and clean in taste, texture, and smell. Packaging that is clean and spare, using predominately white and metallic colors, with an excellent design will capture their attention.

Wood Element people (long rectangular face, sallow complexion, square jaws, full, dark eyebrows, and strong brow bones) are action oriented and often athletic, so their foods reflect the need for high energy. They're the big meat eaters. They favor strong foods—in taste, shapes, textures, and weights. If they do eat veggies, they will be green and have a strong flavor. They also respond to deep green and wood-like images on packaging.

The Fire Element person (oval face, pointed chin, arched eyebrows, flushed skin tones, upward slanted eyes) is very fun-loving, creative, and has a million ideas. The Fire personality always wants fun.

*(continued)*

*(Continued)*

Shopping needs to be fun, the ingredients should be fun, and the eating is always a fun experience. Radiant red, and any other bright color combinations in packaging, as well as in foods, draws their attention. Creative, unusual, fun packaging and presentations will sell the product to a Fire type. Give them lots of spicy foods, exotic tastes, and frequent surprises. They also love sweets, but unlike Earth types who crave sweets as part of their nurturing, comfort-food, the Fire-type craves chocolate because it's rich and exciting and it releases certain endorphins associated with falling in love—which Fire types like to do, a lot!

The Water Element person (round, full face, especially in the mid and lower section, dreamy eyes, dark circles under eyes) is the most yin (inward, feminine—even masculine men can have lots of yin!) and has an aura of mystery. Blue foods of any type—plums, prunes, kidney beans, purple grapes are favorites. Water Element people are very aural, and so respond to the spoken sales pitch, or the written pitch that has a rhythm to it. They are drawn to sensual foods, textures, and packaging, and they favor mysterious black and deep blues.

Let me give an example of how the different Wu Xing types shop, using the Wood type: The Wood type is often very athletic, so it's safe to assume that the food and vitamin stores that cater to body builders and athletes are in essence catering to the Wood type. To better attract them, use a lot of wood in the store (literally and figuratively) for shelving, displays, and counters. And use very little metal (literally and figuratively) as metal cuts the energy of wood. Since Wood types are drawn to tall rectangular shapes (think tall redwood trees, think the build of basketball players), and strong tree-like images, use those shapes and images for display, for posters, for signs on walls, and for packaging. Dark green is associated with growth and strength, and draws the attention of the Wood types.

---

Patricia McCarthy is president of the Mien Shiang Institute of Los Angeles, California, and is recognized as one of the top American authorities in the field.

the attention of a touchy-feely shopper more than a competitive product that did not have the same images and wording. A trip down the bottled-water aisle is a perfect study of how some package designs reach out to the shopper who is more sensitive and attracted to kinesthetics. Clear plastic bottles with waterfalls, streams, and snow-covered ice caps all evoke feelings of pure and fresh water; while the opaque plastic jugs with no photo present a no frills, economy image.

---

*The second lesson is one to be taught to in-store demonstrators. Typically, the in-store demonstration is a relatively passive marketing tool. While it is common for demonstrators to verbally and physically offer a shopper a sample as they are passing the sampling location, most demonstrators are not trained to seek out the shoppers most likely to buy their product.*

---

In fact, what they are trained to do is develop a relationship with the department manager, prepare the product according to its specifications, present it in an attractive way to the shopper, and be cordial. They are not trained or rewarded for being insightful, to be able to offer a sample to the shopper most likely to buy. Instead, they are instructed to sample to as many people as possible.

Demonstrators are instructed by brand managers to sample in locations adjacent to the product's shelf location whenever possible. Another missed opportunity. In many supermarkets, the policy is to sample at the end of the aisle or in more open areas, which both creates visual excitement in the store and prevents traffic congestion. It is in these areas—deli, bakery, produce, or meat—that the demonstrator and the product being featured have the greatest opportunity to attract new customers. Your demonstrator must be tuned in to observe shoppers to see which ones are the most likely candidates to buy your product. A shopper who spends time touching or smelling fruits, comparing packages of wrapped poultry or beef, or smelling a baked good before purchasing it, is the shopper most likely to buy a product that he or she is unfamiliar with through sampling.

Taking the extra time to design the right package and right presentation will help you find the shoppers that will turn into your best and most loyal customers. Let the shoppers' senses do the work for you.

# PART FIVE

# HEALTHY MARKETING

CHAPTER

15

# Diet for Health or Diet for Appearance?

Matthew cares about what he eats. He reads labels, pays attention to the latest food and health reports, and is willing to pay a little extra for those foods that offer health benefits. His dad has diabetes, high blood pressure, and is at least 40 pounds overweight. His mom, a schoolteacher, has always been thin and in great shape; she eats lots of fruits and vegetables, as does Matthew. Recently, his shopping trips are taking more time as he tries to read the ingredient and nutritional facts labels, which seem to be adding more information and claims. He has found that the best (and quickest) way to find out what he needs to know is by asking one of the store clerks. Unlike those in most traditional supermarkets, the clerks in the Whole Foods Supermarket where he shops really

*understand nutrition, and keep up on the latest labeling regula-*
*tions. He has compared prices and finds he is spending almost 15*
*percent more on his groceries. Matthew feels it's a small price to*
*pay for better nutrition and information.*

## "Health, the Open Sesame to the Sucker's Purse"

That's an actual quote, from *The Road to Wellville*, in which
Michael Lerner (playing Goodloe Bender) is trying to convince
John Cusack (playing Charles Ossining), that their brand of corn
flakes—Perfo—could put Dr. John Kellogg's Corn Flakes out of
business. I often use this quote to remind marketers that more is
needed than just a healthy-sounding name or design to attract the
health-oriented shopper. Marketing and appealing to a health-
conscious shopper began many hundreds of years ago, with patent
medicines and would-be healers traveling from town to town
hawking their miracle cures.

According to Tim Hammonds, president and CEO of the Food
Marketing Institute, the old model for health used to be to wait for
an illness, then go to a doctor. The new model is for people to take
an active role in preventing disease and prolonging a healthy, active
life. This means eating for health, as part of a whole health solution, which includes diet, exercise, and healthy lifestyle choices. As
a result, expect more food bioengineered to deliver specific health
benefits, perhaps even replacing many of today's medications.

Shoppers can be attracted to healthy foods for a number of reasons: to lose weight, improve health, prevent illness or diseases, or
due to philosophical or religious belief. Much of your marketing
strategy will depend on just how shoppers see your product. Much
of your long-term success and brand building will be determined by
how you relate to shoppers and what kinds of information you give
them. When it comes to health, the most powerful marketing tool
you have is the truth.

One of the most successfully marketed brands in this newly developing category is Newman's Own Organics. Expanding the Newman's Own brand into organics was the brainchild of daughter Nell and, to convince her parents (Paul Newman and Joanne Woodward) of how good organics were; she cooked an entirely organic Thanksgiving dinner for the family. Launched in 1993, the division (as does Newman's Own) donates 100 percent of after-tax profits to charity. Organic chocolates, pretzels, tortilla chips, cookies, and Fig Newmans are sold in supermarkets and health-food stores nationwide.

"One of the most important things to me," Nell Newman says, "is to realize that in 1920, 80 percent of consumer's food dollar went directly to the farmer, and today it's around 10 percent" (data varies from sources—USDA says its 21 percent). She credits chefs for demystifying organics and heralds the growth in farmers markets, which allow consumers to actually communicate and learn from the farmers themselves. Having access to foods that are grown locally and have not been shipped 100 miles is a good thing. While having a famous face on the label certainly doesn't hurt, the success of Newman's Own Organics can be credited to the unending commitment to organic agriculture. Through the products' packaging and media exposure, Nell Newman presents her case to the shopper in a manner that is straightforward and honest. The result is a strong consumer and retailer loyalty to the brand.

Not all products enjoy that shopper relationship, no matter how healthy they may be. Soy milk is a perfect example of how nutrition research and discovery—coupled with a strong consumer desire—has built a new category. Brand loyalty and imagery seems far behind consumption. In a summer 2001 SupermarketGuru.com Consumer Panel, we surveyed over 3,000 visitors to the site about soy milk. Over 62 percent of the group had tried soy milk, with 53 percent (1,620 consumers) who consumed soy milk on a regular basis. When queried about the brands they prefer or use, there was no measurable difference or loyalty among the brands. In fact, when asked which brand name soy milk they used or preferred, over 30 percent of the

Coldbuster, Powerboost, Pro Arobek Plus, Dr. Robeks, Hangover Over, or Healthy Healer, are all clever brand names you might expect to see in a homeopathic pharmacy or health-food store. They conjure up improved health and, for some, the cure-all or fountain of youth. In fact, these are just a few of the hundreds of different names that juice bars are giving their nutrition-supplement-enhanced beverages. It's great marketing and, no doubt, increases brand loyalty and drives sales.

You may wonder, which shoppers are going to these juice bars and buying these fortified drinks? Aging baby boomers that want to stay young. Fitness buffs that want to get the most out of their nutritional intake and exercise. Dieters who want to make sure they get a good balance of protein and nutrients as they cut their caloric intake. Families who just want to get a cool and healthy nutritious drink. The bottom line is that this is one of the few categories that is attracting a wide audience.

There is a sound consumer-based need behind the trend of juice bars (unlike that of a coffee bar, for example). The average American today consumes less than three servings per day of fruit and vegetables, well short of the minimum five servings recommended by the USDA Nutrition Guidelines. If preparing fruits and vegetables for our meals is too much trouble for many of us, isn't it easier to just mix them up and drink them? The answer seems to be yes.

According to Kirk Perron, Chairman of Jamba Juice, about 98 percent of people who are served at Jamba order their beverage with at least one supplement (all smoothies at Jamba include one free boost, additional ones can be added for 50 cents each. The favorite? Vita Juice Boost™, which contains 20 different vitamins and minerals and is described as "100 percent daily value of 20 vital vitamins & minerals for total health."

Estimates are that almost 300 juice bars are open for business in Southern California where the trend started and, according to Jamba Juice, that translates to about $100 million dollars in sales. Nationwide, he says, sales should reach $1 billion dollars in 2001 at establishments with names like Jamba Juice, Robek's, Frozen Fusion, Jumpin' Juice & Java, and Planet Smoothie.

respondents wrote in the flavor or color of the package instead of the brand.

## Who's Eating Organic, Anyway?

A new consumer survey on organic consumption might well be showing marketers the pathway to long-term success. The Walnut Acres Certified Organic Future National Consumer Survey (so called, as Walnut Acres sponsored the July 2, 2001 Roper Starch Report) underscores the fact that consumers are more confused than ever about organics. It's this finding, while certainly not new, that should be the wake up call for both organic brands and retailers that it's now or never.

The survey reports that 63 percent of the respondents feel that organic foods and beverages are better and more healthful for them than nonorganics. So, the astute retailer might ask, why isn't that reflected in what shoppers buy?

The Walnut Acres Survey does point us in quite a few directions that can help resolve the dilemma. The survey found that three out of four consumers (75%) were not able to differentiate between organic foods and those that are labeled all-natural.

While a boon for marketers and products that position themselves as healthy, the time has come for honest and clear labeling, as American shoppers are getting smarter and more concerned about their health. If supermarkets truly want to become whole health centers, it'll be critical to understand just what the consumer is saying—and this survey has the best snapshot of the industry to date.

The survey finds that 79 percent are concerned about the safety of their foods, particularly growth hormones, pesticide residue, bacterial contamination, and genetic modification, a statistic that we can expect to see popping up everywhere as the controversy surrounding genetically modified organisms (GMO) labeling continues.

**Be the Shopper**
Being healthy doesn't have to mean low calorie or low fat. Amy's Kitchen is one of my favorite brands of foods. Rachel and Andy Berliner started the company based on two simple premises: being organic and tasting great. When I interview shoppers who are concerned about their health, Amy's brand always comes up. When I ask them if they are concerned about the extra calories and fat, they smile and tell me that eating Amy's organic foods with a little extra of both is a lot healthier than the way they used to eat.

Little surprise that eight in ten said that they would be more likely to buy products with the new USDA organic seal, rather than organic products without the label. We have long felt that while the new USDA regulations are a substantial step in the right direction, having multiple designations for varying quantities of organic ingredients is more confusing than helpful. Once again we will predict that those products with 100 percent certified organic ingredients and the USDA seal will be those that build this industry. Those that contain organic ingredients mixed with nonorganics will do more to confuse consumers than help.

While the survey reports that 63 percent of adults do sometimes buy organics, the challenge for this industry is to get more items purchased, more often. As organic products themselves continue to move out of the fringe into more mainstream flavors and recipes, there is little question that more consumers will try (and like) the products. As the 2002 labeling deadline grows near, brands should review their ingredients and try to meet the standard for the 100 percent USDA organic seal, otherwise the potential for this category may never be realized.

*Matthew never ate organic foods until he started dating Jennifer. Each Sunday, they would drive to an organic farmer's market and spend the afternoon selecting from the produce stands. He found that the fruits and vegetables they bought there did taste better. He wasn't sure if it was because they had just been picked or because*

---

---

*they were organic, but he really didn't care. What convinced him to buy organic was that Jennifer told him that buying certified organic foods was the only way to avoid genetically modified food.*

## Take Your Pick: The Marketing of Frankenstein Foods or Marketing Cures for Disease?

Nutrition is a relatively new science. As a result, new research often contradicts either decades-old conventional wisdom or another scientist's findings that might be less than a year old. As a result, shoppers are more confused and cautious (as they should be) about the foods they consume. Nowhere is this more apparent than in the current controversy surrounding genetically modified organisms. The marketing stage was set in June 1999, when Prince Charles, in his regular newspaper editorial in the *Daily Mail*, cautioned the public to be concerned about the impending genetic food movements. He named these foods *Frankenstein foods,* and the term has become as powerful as a brand to consumers worldwide.

Much of the science, or lack thereof, has been pushed to the side by both consumer groups and industry associations that continue to fight over whether or not these foods should be labeled. Labeling a food genetically modified is not required and, although this regulation is currently being reviewed at this time, it is doubtful that the law will change. The American supermarket shopper is used to having choice and reading labels. Being able to identify GMO ingredients and trace them to their source is not as difficult as many of the trade organizations present it to be. Philip J. Regal, PhD, professor of ecology, evolution, and behavior in the College of Biological Sciences at the University of Minnesota, one of the experts who presented at the FDA's biotechnology hearings stated: "It is not a question if it can be done. The question is whether we want to."

Based on five SupermarketGuru.com Consumer Panel Surveys throughout 2001, we report that consumers want the information that will tell them whether a product or ingredient has been genetically modified. They site a multitude of reasons: allergies, long-term health effects, politics, religious beliefs, or just choice. Currently, the regulation mandates that any foods that are derived from new plant varieties that are produced through biotechnology would be regulated in the same fashion as those created through traditional means: the Federal Food, Drug, and Cosmetic Act. That means all the products are evaluated for their individual safety, allergenicity, and toxicity. However, if the food is derived from uncharacteristic genetic elements, the FDA requires it to go through a full food safety evaluation.

Genetic engineering is the process that splices genetic material from a source, like plants, animals, or bacteria, into the DNA of other organisms. USDA estimates are that in 2000, genetically engineered crops comprised over 25 percent of the U.S. cropland, which includes 35 percent of all corn, 55 percent of all soybeans, and 50 percent of all cotton.

**Be the Shopper**

**In 2002, American farmers will plant more genetically engineered crops than ever before. The Agriculture Department reports that a 13 percent increase will translate to one-third of all corn on U.S. soil being genetically modified. The question is whether international and American consumer resistance will force labeling of these foods.**

The thought of the new biotech food technologies might well stir up images in many shoppers' minds of the film *Soylent Green*, and reducing mealtime to a single pill, but the truth is that a lot of our foods are getting healthier. Some innovations are coming to market because of science, and some as people head back to the basics of good nutrition.

This new food language is being created with words like *biotech genetically engineered foods* and *functional foods,* confusing to shoppers. Most American consumers have no awareness of the genetically engineered foods they are consuming. A recent survey by the

International Food Information Council found that two-thirds of Americans were unaware that genetically engineered foods are available in the supermarket.

---

*It's how we educate and market this next generation*
*of foods that will make the difference between*
*success and failure.*

---

The opportunity for functional foods that may or may not be derived through genetic modification seems to be the one all can agree on. These foods, sometimes referred to as *nutraceuticals* or *designer foods,* "contain substantial elements providing physiological benefits that can enhance physical well-being when combined with a healthy lifestyle," according to the Grocery Manufacturers Association. The fact is that we are now seeing products, after approval and verification of the FDA, that can actually make health claims and prevent disease. Oats that lower cholesterol and reduce the risk of some cancers, and margarine and salad dressings that lower cholesterol are just a few now on supermarket shelves; we can expect much more to come.

Weight-loss products and diet programs (estimated to be a $35 billion market in the United States in 2001), especially supplements in pill or powder form, use both talk radio and print ads to promise quick weight loss. As shoppers learn about the latest diets . . . do you know enough to sell them the foods they want?

Most shoppers want to look good, and looking good is certainly one of the reasons for the phenomenal growth in the diet category but more important is the fact that over 50 percent of the U.S. population is considered overweight or obese, even with all the diet foods and miracle cures. There are literally tons of diet books on the market—a keyword search for "weight loss" on Amazon.com revealed 1,214 matches. Of the top 50 best-selling diet books of all time, 58 percent were published in 1999 or 2000, and 88 percent were published since 1997.

## The Information Is Out There, It's Just Not Getting Through

Many supermarkets have tried to build relationships with their customers through nutrition classes, store tours, and cooking classes—all admirable efforts that have helped countless customers. Usually, however, it's an outside registered dietitian or health professional that is knowledgeable about diets. For supermarkets to capture the whole-health solution positioning that so many are now targeting, the information must be shared among store-level personnel that come in contact with customers.

According to the USDA, most people trying to lose weight are going about it incorrectly, and are not following the recommended combination of reducing caloric intake and increasing physical activity. In a recently published study about popular diets, over 70 percent of respondents reported using each of the following strategies at least once in four years: increased exercise, decreased fat intake, reduced food amount, and reduced calories, although the duration of any one of these behaviors was usually brief.

Marketers that want to attract shoppers to their products based on a diet strategy should follow the path of least resistance, and develop and position their brands into the already-established diet categories that shoppers know.

- High-fat, low-carbohydrate, high-protein diets. Some examples are *Dr. Atkins' New Diet Revolution, Protein Power,* and *Life Without Bread.*

- Moderate-fat reduction diets. These are high in carbohydrates and moderate in protein. Some examples are the USDA Food Guide Pyramid, DASH diet, and Weight Watchers.

- Low-fat and very low fat, very high-carbohydrate, moderate-protein diets. The examples are *Dr. Dean Ornish's Program for Reversing Heart Disease; Eat More, Weigh Less* (also by Ornish); and *The New Pritikin Program.*

---

**WHICH DIETS WORK, ACCORDING TO THE USDA**

- Studies show that high-protein diets similar to the Atkins' diets do result in weight loss. Individuals consuming high-fat, low-carbohydrate diets may lose weight because the intake of protein and fat is self-limiting, and overall calorie intake is decreased.

- Moderate fat-reduction diets contain moderate amounts of carbohydrate and protein. When overall caloric intake is reduced, these diets result in loss of body weight and body fat.

- Low-fat and very low-fat diets contain a high proportion of complex carbohydrates, fruits, and vegetables. They are naturally high in fiber and low in caloric density. Individuals participating in these types of diets consume fewer calories and lose weight.

---

Today's shoppers understand that excess weight is associated with increased mortality and cardiovascular disease, type 2 diabetes, hypertension, stroke, gall bladder disease, osteoarthritis, sleep apnea and respiratory problems, and certain types of cancer. They are more willing to try products that make weight loss easy and painless. However, marketers have a responsibility if they want to build a strong brand relationship and be a primary source of food and wellness, especially when it comes to dieting, brands, and the information they transmit. All their communication channels, advertising, and packaging must be competent and honest to satisfy the shopper's need for knowledge and product.

CHAPTER
16

# The Dos and Don'ts of Marketing Health Claims

## Truth in Labeling. What a Concept!

Consumer groups, including the Center for Science in the Public Interest and the Food Allergy Network, have been urging manufacturers for decades to clean up ingredient labels. One reason is that more consumers seem to be affected by an increasing number of food allergies. Some blame the environment, some blame our farming practices, and some blame the rise of genetically modified organisms (GMOs).

Whatever the source, it turns out that many consumers are more aware of food allergies than ever before, and more careful about what they eat. This translates to a unique brand building opportunity for many products. While there are the nay sayers who dispute whether these allergies are real or imagined, the fact is that there are consumers whose lives or general health can be threatened by consuming the wrong ingredient; they are reading labels carefully, looking for brands they can trust.

According to the Food and Drug Administration (FDA), food allergies affect an estimated six to seven million consumers in the United States. Currently, there are no cures for food allergies, and the only successful method to manage these allergies is to avoid foods that contain the causative agents. However, too often, ingredient listings have not been complete enough to serve as an effective tool for consumers.

One of the problems for marketers is that the FDA has not formally defined *allergens*, but it has listed the foods that are the most commonly known to cause serious allergenic responses. Ninety percent or more of all food allergies are caused by the proteins from the foods listed here:

- Crustaceans (e.g., crab, lobster, and shrimp)
- Eggs
- Fish
- Milk
- Peanuts
- Soy
- Tree nuts (almonds, Brazil nuts, cashews, chestnuts, filberts, hazelnuts, macadamia nuts, pecans, pine nuts, pistachios, and walnuts)
- Wheat

The new Food Allergen Labeling Guidelines, which are being promoted by the industry, rather than being regulated by the FDA, are designed to inform shoppers in easy to understand language. One major flaw of the current FDA regulation is the requirement to use scientific terms on the label, for example, listing albumin for eggs

---

#### FOOD ALLERGEN LABELING GUIDELINES

Product packages will now include the designation, "contains _____," with the allergen listed in immediate proximity to the ingredient declaration. For example, { + } "Contains soy and milk."

An ingredient that contains one of the major food allergens would be designated by an asterisk referring the consumer to a statement of explanation. For example, "whey" would be listed as "whey*" and would be followed by "*milk" after the complete ingredient declaration. { + } Ingredients: Sugar, chocolate, whey*, coconut, *milk.

Flavors that are now listed as *natural flavors*, will be listed as "natural flavors (peanuts and soy)" or as { + } "natural peanut flavor" and "natural soy flavor."

---

or whey for milk, which can be confusing. That will be changed, so that commonly understood terms will be used. Foods that contain a protein of one of these major food allergens will also appear on the label if it is contained in a flavor.

In July 2000, the U.S. General Accounting Office (GAO) issued their long awaited report, titled "Improvements Needed in Overseeing the Safety of Dietary Supplements and Functional Foods." This report was prepared in response to the rapidly expanding consumer demand for these supplement products, coupled with a series of complaints (numbering 2,797 since 1993, including 105 deaths) about the adverse effects of some dietary supplements.

The FDA describes *nutritional supplements* as products that "claim to have health benefits beyond basic nutrition" and *nutraceuticals* (as a smoothie with supplements would be defined), as products that "have the basic attributes of traditional foods—taste, aroma, or nutritive value—and that claim to provide an additional health benefit." According to the GAO, last year Americans spent about $31 billion on these types of products, and diet aids alone, according to AC Nielsen, amounted to $911 million in the year ending February 24, 1992.

# The Marketing of Health Claims

Health claims authorized by the FDA are one of several ways food labels can win the attention of health-conscious consumers. Under the Nutrition Labeling and Education Act of 1990, the FDA has approved 10 health claims for use in food labeling thus far. The idea is that health claims should show a relationship between a nutrient or other substance in a food, and a disease or health condition. These claims can be used on conventional food or dietary supplements.

Health claims differ from the more common claims that highlight a food's nutritional content, such as *low fat* or *high fiber*. They are also different from so-called structure/function claims, for example, "Calcium builds strong bones." Unlike health claims, structure/function claims do not deal with disease risk reduction and are not approved or authorized by the FDA.

We discuss the FDA-authorized health claims and some specifics about their use next.

## Calcium and Osteoporosis

Low calcium intake is one risk factor for osteoporosis, a condition of reduced bone mass, or density. Lifelong adequate calcium intake helps maintain bone mass by increasing, as much as genetically possible, the amount of bone formed in the teens and early adult years, and by helping to slow the rate of bone loss that occurs later in life.

*Typical Foods.* Low-fat and skim milk, yogurt, tofu, calcium-fortified citrus drinks, some calcium supplements, canned sardines and salmon (with bones), and many dark leafy greens including spinach and kale.

*Requirements.* Food or supplement must be high in calcium, and not contain more phosphorus than calcium. Claims must cite other risk factors, state the need for regular exercise and a healthful diet, explain that adequate calcium early in life helps reduce fracture risk later by increasing as much as genetically possible a person's peak bone mass, and indicate that those at greatest risk of developing osteoporosis later in life are white and Asian teenage and young adult women, who are in their bone-forming years. Claims for products with more than 400 mg calcium per day must state that a daily intake of over 2,000 mg offers no added known benefit to bone health.

*Sample Claim.* "Regular exercise and a healthy diet with enough calcium helps teen and young adult white and Asian women maintain good bone health, and may reduce their high risk of osteoporosis later in life."

## Sodium and Hypertension (High Blood Pressure)

Hypertension is a risk factor for coronary heart disease and stroke deaths. The most common source of sodium is table salt. Diets low in sodium may help lower blood pressure and related risks in many people. Guidelines recommend a daily sodium intake of not more than 2,400 mg. Typical U.S. intake ranges from 3,000 to 6,000 mg.

*Typical Foods.* Unsalted tuna, salmon, fruits and vegetables, low-fat milk, low-fat yogurt, cottage cheese, sherbet, ice milk, cereal, flour, and pasta (not egg pasta).

*Requirements.* Foods must meet criteria for low sodium. Claims must use *sodium* and *high blood pressure* in discussing the nutrient–disease link.

*Sample Claim.* "Diets low in sodium may reduce the risk of high blood pressure, a disease associated with many factors."

## Dietary Fat and Cancer

Diets high in fat increase the risk of some types of cancer, such as breast, colon, and prostate. While scientists don't know how total fat intake affects cancer development, low-fat diets reduce the risk. Experts recommend that Americans consume 30 percent or less of their daily calories as fat. Typical U.S. intake is 37 percent.

*Typical Foods.* Fruits, vegetables, reduced-fat milk products, cereal, pasta, flour, and sherbet.

*Requirements.* Foods must meet criteria for low fat. Fish and game meats must meet criteria for extra lean. Claims may not mention specific types of fats and must use *total fat* or *fat* and *some types of cancer* or *some cancers* in discussing the nutrient–disease link.

*Sample Claim.* "Development of cancer depends on many factors. A diet low in total fat may reduce the risk of some cancers."

## Dietary Saturated Fat and Cholesterol and Risk of Coronary Heart Disease

Diets high in saturated fat and cholesterol increase total and low-density (bad) blood cholesterol levels and, thus, the risk of coronary heart disease. Diets low in saturated fat and cholesterol decrease this risk. Guidelines recommend that American diets contain less than 10 percent of calories from saturated fat, and less than 300 mg cholesterol daily. The average American adult diet contains 13 percent saturated fat, and 300 to 400 mg cholesterol per day.

*Typical Foods.* Fruits, vegetables, skim and low-fat milk, cereal, whole-grain products, and pasta (not egg pasta).

*Requirements.* Foods must meet criteria for low saturated fat, low cholesterol, and low fat. Fish and game meats must meet criteria for extra lean. Claims must use *saturated fat and cholesterol* and *coronary heart disease* or *heart disease* in discussing the nutrient–disease link.

*Sample Claim.* "While many factors affect heart disease, diets low in saturated fat and cholesterol may reduce the risk of this disease."

## Fiber-Containing Grain Products, Fruits, and Vegetables, and Cancer

Diets low in fat and rich in fiber-containing grain products, fruits, and vegetables may reduce the risk of some types of cancer. The exact role of total dietary fiber, fiber components, and other nutrients and substances in these foods is not fully understood.

*Typical Foods.* Whole-grain bread and cereal, fruits, and vegetables.

*Requirements.* Foods must meet criteria for low fat and, without fortification, be a good source of dietary fiber. Claims must not specify types of fiber and must use *fiber, dietary fiber,* or *total dietary fiber* and *some types of cancer* or *some cancers* in discussing the nutrient–disease link.

*Sample Claim.* "Low-fat diets rich in fiber-containing grain products, fruits, and vegetables may reduce the risk of some types of cancer, a disease associated with many factors."

## Fruits, Vegetables, and Grain Products That Contain Fiber, Particularly Soluble Fiber, and Risk of Coronary Heart Disease

Diets low in saturated fat and cholesterol and rich in fruits, vegetables, and grain products that contain fiber, particularly soluble fiber, may reduce the risk of coronary heart disease. (It is impossible to adequately distinguish the effects of fiber, including soluble fiber, from those of other food components.)

*Typical Foods.* Fruits, vegetables, and whole-grain bread and cereal.

*Requirements.* Foods must meet criteria for low saturated fat, low fat, and low cholesterol. They must contain, without fortification, at least 0.6 g of soluble fiber per reference amount, and the soluble fiber content must be listed. Claims must use *fiber, dietary fiber, some types of dietary fiber, some dietary fibers,* or *some fibers,* and *coronary heart disease* or *heart disease* in discussing the nutrient–disease link. The term *soluble fiber* may be added.

*Sample Claim.* "Diets low in saturated fat and cholesterol and rich in fruits, vegetables, and grain products that contain some types of dietary fiber, particularly soluble fiber, may reduce the risk of heart disease, a disease associated with many factors."

## Fruits and Vegetables and Cancer

Diets low in fat and rich in fruits and vegetables may reduce the risk of some cancers. Fruits and vegetables are low-fat foods, and may contain fiber or vitamin A (as beta-carotene) and vitamin C. (The effects of these vitamins cannot be adequately distinguished from those of other fruit or vegetable components.)

*Typical Foods.* Fruits and vegetables.

*Requirements.* Foods must meet criteria for low fat and, without fortification, be a good source of fiber, vitamin A, or vitamin C. Claims must characterize fruits and vegetables as foods that are low in fat and may contain dietary fiber, vitamin A, or vitamin C; characterize the food itself as a good source of one or more of these nutrients, which must be listed; refrain from specifying types of fatty acids; and use *total* fat or *fat, some types of cancer,* or *some* cancers, and *fiber, dietary fiber,* or *total dietary fiber* in discussing the nutrient–disease link.

*Sample Claim.* "Low-fat diets rich in fruits and vegetables (foods that are low in fat and may contain dietary fiber, vitamin A, or vitamin C) may reduce the risk of some types of cancer, a disease associated with many factors. Broccoli is high in vitamins A and C, and is a good source of dietary fiber."

## Folate and Neural Tube Birth Defects

Defects of the neural tube (a structure that develops into the brain and spinal cord) occur within the first six weeks after conception, often before the pregnancy is known. The U.S. Public Health Service recommends that all women of childbearing age in the United States consume 0.4 mg (400 mcg) of folic acid daily to reduce their risk of having a baby affected with spina bifida or other neural tube defects.

*Typical Foods.* Enriched cereal grain products, some legumes (dried beans), peas, fresh leafy-green vegetables, oranges, grapefruit, many berries, some dietary supplements, and fortified breakfast cereal.

*Requirements.* Foods must meet or exceed criteria for being a good source of folate, that is, at least 40 mcg folic acid per serving (at least 10 percent of the daily value). A serving of food cannot contain more than 100 percent of the daily value for vitamin A and vitamin D, because of their potential risk to fetuses. Claims must use *folate, folic acid,* or *folacin,* and *neural tube defects, birth defects, spina bifida or anencephaly, birth defects of the brain or spinal cord, anencephaly, or spina bifida, spina bifida and anencephaly, birth defects of the brain or spinal cord, birth defects of the brain and spinal cord,* or *brain or spinal cord birth defects* in discussing the nutrient–disease link. Folic acid content must be listed on the nutrition facts panel.

*Sample Claim.*    "Healthful diets with adequate folate may reduce a woman's risk of having a child with a brain or spinal cord birth defect."

## Dietary Sugar Alcohol and Dental Caries (Cavities)

Between-meal eating of foods high in sugar and starches may promote tooth decay. Sugarless candies made with certain sugar alcohols do not.

*Typical Foods.*    Sugarless candy and gum.

*Requirements.*    Foods must meet the criteria for sugar free. The sugar alcohol must be xylitol, sorbitol, mannitol, maltitol, isomalt, lactitol, hydrogenated starch hydrolysates, hydrogenated glucose syrups, erythritol, or a combination of these. When the food contains a fermentable carbohydrate, such as sugar or flour, the food must not lower plaque pH in the mouth below 5.7 while it is being eaten, or up to 30 minutes afterward. Claims must use *sugar alcohol, sugar alcohols,* or the name(s) of the sugar alcohol present, and *dental caries* or *tooth decay* in discussing the nutrient–disease link. Claims must state that the sugar alcohol present *does not promote, may reduce the risk of, is useful in not promoting,* or *is expressly for not promoting* dental caries.

*Sample Claim.*    Full claim: "Frequent between-meal consumption of foods high in sugars and starches promotes tooth decay. The sugar alcohols in this food do not promote tooth decay." Shortened claim (on small packages only): "Does not promote tooth decay."

## Dietary Soluble Fiber, Such as That Found in Whole Oats and Psyllium Seed Husk, and Coronary Heart Disease

When included in a diet low in saturated fat and cholesterol, soluble fiber may affect blood lipid levels, such as cholesterol, and thus lower the risk of heart disease. However, because soluble dietary fibers constitute a family of heterogeneous substances that vary greatly in their effect on the risk of heart disease, the FDA has determined that sources of soluble fiber for this health claim need to be considered on a case-by-case basis. To date, the FDA has reviewed and authorized two sources of soluble fiber eligible for this claim: whole oats and psyllium seed husk.

*Typical Foods.* Oatmeal cookies, muffins, bread and other foods made with rolled oats, oat bran, or whole oat flour; hot and cold breakfast cereal containing whole oats or psyllium seed husk; and dietary supplements containing psyllium seed husk.

*Requirements.* Foods must meet criteria for low saturated fat, low cholesterol, and low fat. Foods that contain whole oats must contain at least 0.75 g soluble fiber per serving. Foods that contain psyllium seed husk must contain at least 1.7 g soluble fiber per serving. The claim must specify the daily dietary intake of the soluble fiber source necessary to reduce the risk of heart disease and the contribution one serving of the product makes toward that intake level. Soluble fiber content must be stated in the nutrition label. Claims must use *soluble fiber,* qualified by the name of the eligible source of soluble fiber, and *heart disease* or *coronary heart disease* in discussing the nutrient–disease link. Because of the potential hazard of choking, foods containing dry or incompletely hydrated psyllium seed husk must carry a label statement telling consumers to drink adequate amounts of fluid, unless the manufacturer shows that a viscous adhesive mass is not formed when the food is exposed to fluid.

*Sample Claim.* "Diets low in saturated fat and cholesterol that include 3 g soluble fiber from whole oats per day may reduce the risk of heart disease. One serving of this whole-oats product provides 3 grams of this soluble fiber."

# CONCLUSION

# A Marketing Philosophy to Share

*Maureen and Janie, the only two female members of Ten-Den are also the only two who ever care about which foods they eat. They read labels and they count calories. The four guys are typical preteens, who eat anything within reach. Doug and Lupe are already at least 20 pounds overweight. The other two burn the calories they eat; Tao is into playing basketball, and Joe rides his bike three miles to school each day. The Ten-Den are smart; each member is a straight-A student. Their primary supply of food, besides their own homes, is the convenience store. Maureen and Joe go shopping with their moms occasionally, but the others can't remember the last time they were in a full-size supermarket. The four aisles in the convenience store limit their food and beverage brand and product universe. Their choices are made by brand names and accessibility.*

*Being the Shopper* is more than the marketing strategy of the moment. It is a guide to a philosophy and way of thinking that forces brand managers and CEOs and everyone involved in products sold in the supermarket to focus on the shopper.

In this book, I have shared the learning and experience that have come from twenty-five years of consumer interviews, and millions of miles walked on hard supermarket floors. I have learned that marketing and advertising at their best join the right people with the right brands and, at their worst, fill cupboards with products that are never used and build consumer resentment.

Understanding the consumer is important, but understanding how a consumer behaves during a shopping experience and why they behave this way is critical. The information contained in *Being the Shopper* is not just for food companies. Every company must follow consumer trends and understand how these trends affect their businesses. *Being the Shopper* is a guidebook for all companies. Understanding people's behaviors is relevant to all businesses and all products and services.

This book is meant to be shared. No great marketing ideas are kept secret. Disseminating the ideas and tools that are contained within these pages will make brands and companies stronger, and those marketers who share them are destined to lead our consumer products businesses to success.

You are reading the last pages of this book, but if I have done my job well, these pages will start you on a new marketing journey—a journey led by a new passion and one full of consumer emotions to explore.

I leave you for now with just one more list to help guide you down the yellow brick road of marketing:

---

### THE TOP TEN WAYS TO BE THE SHOPPER

1. Learning how to listen to shoppers is the most important and effective marketing tool you can ever possess and, unlike an advertising strategy or new idea, it can never be stolen or taken away.

*(Continued)*

2. Marketing, advertising, and brand communications are there to sell products and build a relationship with consumers. Always question if the message is getting through, and use sales to measure to what degree.

3. New product introductions are destined for failure. Unless your new product idea is truly unique and proprietary, spend your time and money building your current brands and products.

4. Train yourself to separate what you like from what you think shoppers will like.

5. Spend a half day every month answering consumer calls or e-mails to your brand. Don't use the prewritten responses, instead, write new ones, no matter how difficult or how much research it will take. The process will force you to learn how to improve your product.

6. Keep your products in front of you; on your desk where you can see and touch them. Be the caretaker of your brand and leave your brand better than you found it.

7. E-commerce is here to stay. Buy three food products online at least once a month from three different Web sites, and track how the technology is improving the shopping experience. Read about the innovations in technology on software-developer Web sites and in computer magazines.

8. Think holistically: Understand that the ways in which you communicate and attract shoppers is multidimensional. Every word, color, phrase, claim, and ingredient makes a difference. Communicate holistically: Be as visual, auditory, and kinesthetic in every communication and advertisement as you can.

9. Understand that today's shoppers are different than they will be tomorrow, and focus on where they are going, instead of where they have been.

10. Visit at least five supermarkets each week and talk to at least three shoppers in each. Don't ask them about your product, look to see what is in their shopping cart and ask them why they bought what they did.

There is little doubt in my mind that the new businesses and products that will be created by biotechnology and the new nutrition sciences will have a dramatic impact on consumers. Mapping the genome and having DNA explained in evening newscasts has taken a lot of the fear out of human science. However, understanding the place of DNA in our food supply is less clear and less understood. Researchers' next step is to find those triggers to current and future health and nutrition problems, and turn those genes off, through either surgery or the foods we consume. With these discoveries will come marketing communications' biggest challenge.

Within five years, we will see the technology that will identify your lifetime of health and wellness. The food-and-beverage intake guidelines to ensure a life free from disease and chronic illness will be available at birth. Shoppers will be divided into three distinct groups: those who know about their body's predispositions and choose to use the information to insure a healthy life, those who know but ignore the remedies, and those who choose not to know and live their lives without a DNA blueprint as their guide. No doubt shopping will also change, and give reality to a one-to-one food relationship.

Are you prepared?

# A MARKETING TIME LINE OF KEY SUPERMARKET EVENTS IN THE TWENTIETH CENTURY

1900   Lysol becomes the first antiseptic available to physicians.

1901   Satori Kato develops instant coffee, and markets it at the Pan American Expo in Buffalo, New York.

1902   Nabisco introduces Barnum's Animal Crackers. The box, made to resemble a circus cage, came with a string attached to hang it from a Christmas tree. It made the product a huge success.

1903   James Kraft develops a method to pasteurize cheese, and creates what is now known as American cheese.

1904   Americans are introduced to the hamburger, hot dog, ice-cream cone, iced tea, and French's mustard, all at the 1904 St. Louis World's Fair.

1906   *The Jungle*, by Upton Sinclair, is published, and creates the nation's first food safety uproar.

1907   Scott Paper Company introduces the first paper towel.

1908   Cracker Jack and the Dixie Cup are introduced.

1912    Nabisco introduces the Oreo cookie and George Hellman starts packaging mayonnaise, made from his wife's recipe.

1916    The first mechanical home refrigerators are sold.

1917    Gooch Foods opens the first U.S. pasta-manufacturing plant.

1919    Quaker Oats develops the first instant oatmeal.

1920    The Baby Ruth candy bar (named for Grover Cleveland's daughter) is introduced, and thousands of sample bars are dropped from planes in Pittsburgh.

1921    Betty Crocker, one of the first fictional food celebrities, begins answering consumer letters for Gold Medal Flour.

1923    Wheaties, the breakfast of champions, is introduced by the first singing radio commercial, on *Nick Armstrong's All-American Boy* program. Frank Mars markets the Milky Way candy bar.

1925    The Jolly Green Giant starts appearing on canned vegetables.

1927    Borden introduces homogenized milk; Kellogg's introduces Rice Krispies; and Daniel Gerber starts distributing his wife's idea for strained baby foods.

1930    Clarence Birdseye starts selling Birdseye Frosted Foods. Continental Bakery invents the first sliced bread, and calls it Wonder. The same year, the company also introduces the Hostess Twinkie.

1931    Single-serving boxed pies are sold under the brand Tastykake, and marketed with the slogan "The cake that made Mother stop baking."

1932    Elmer Doolin buys a recipe for tortilla chips for $100, and starts producing Fritos.

1937    Sylvan Goldman invents the grocery shopping cart, so his Humpty Dumpty and Standard Food Market customers could purchase more items than would fit in their hand-held wicker baskets.

1941   American Maize-Products develops genetically modified corn. The first Daily Recommended Dietary Allowances are published.

1946   Procter & Gamble introduces the first heavy-duty laundry detergent—Tide. General Foods gives us Minute Rice, and R.T. French markets the first packaged, dehydrated potatoes as Instant Potatoes.

1947   Reynolds Wrap aluminum foil is introduced.

1948   The first Pillsbury Bake-Off is held in New York City.

1951   S&H Green Stamps are first given away in King Sooper in Denver.

1952   Kellogg's introduces Tony the Tiger and Sugar Frosted Flakes. Mrs. Paul's Fish Sticks start appearing in supermarkets' frozen food departments.

1953   Swift introduces Butterball, the first self-basting turkey. Cheez Whiz is introduced.

1954   C. A. Swanson & Sons introduces the frozen "TV" dinner, which sells for 98 cents and is advertised on television on *The Milton Berle Show* and *Peter Gunn*. Pillsbury starts selling prepared dough in tubes that pop open when smacked against the kitchen counter.

1955   The first home microwave oven is manufactured.

1956   The USDA formulates and announces the four Basic Food groups.

1962   Coca-Cola introduces Tab, Pepsi quickly responds with Diet Pepsi, and a new generation of soft drinks is born.

1963   Weight Watchers has its first meeting. The first spreadable margarine, Chiffon, is introduced.

1965   Researchers at the University of Florida develop Gatorade, named for the school's mascot, the Florida Gator.

1966   The first supermarket consumer food price boycott is recorded in Denver.

1967   Cool Whip, the world's first nondairy whipped topping, is introduced.

1970   L'eggs Pantyhose goes to market in egg-shaped containers, and is sold in supermarkets, changing the way and place women shop for hosiery. Annual beef consumption hits a record high of 113 pounds per person.

1971   Ziploc plastic bags are introduced.

1972   Supermarkets begin scanning by using the Universal Product Code (UPC), which promised shorter lines, and resulted in the removal of individually priced packages.

1981   Stouffer Foods introduces a new concept—an entire line of low-calorie foods called Lean Cuisine.

1986   New Coke and Classic Coke are introduced. Within the year, New Coke is removed from store shelves.

1988   The first Wal-Mart Superstore opens.

1990   Peapod launches home delivery service featuring "Pea Pickers," who promise to select your fresh foods better than you can yourself.

1991   Dollar sales of salsa exceed those of ketchup.

1992   The USDA introduces Food Guide Pyramid.

1993   The annual per capita beef consumption drops to record low of 65.1 pounds.

1994   Nutritional Facts labels are made mandatory on food packages.

1996   Frito Lay introduces WOW!, the first fat-free potato chips, made with Olestra.

1999   Johnson & Johnson introduces Benecol Margarine, the first proven nutraceutical, which lowers cholesterol.

# ACKNOWLEDGMENTS

There is little difference between writing a book and creating the next billion-dollar brand. Both efforts start with a single sound idea, and evolve as trusted and insightful advisors, friends, family, colleagues, and strangers add their input, thoughts, and ideas to help shape the path to success. To all these people that I have worked with throughout my career, and all the shoppers that I have stopped midway through their shopping trips, I offer my thanks for making *Being the Shopper* possible. There is no doubt that, without their help, I would not have the tools to be as committed to understanding the needs of supermarket shoppers.

There are many people acknowledged publicly for their success and expertise within these pages, but there are many behind the scenes who deserve much recognition.

Laura B. Gray, my wife and most valued critic, for spending countless hours reading, rereading, and adding her intelligence to my work.

Kathy Nisivoccia, with whom I will soon share and celebrate a twenty-year collegial anniversary, adds her insight and hard work to all that I do.

Michael Sansolo and Dagmar Farr of the FMI, who are ever present to discuss, challenge, then reinforce my ideas about shoppers and their supermarkets.

Amy Chen, our nutritionist, researched and wrote portions of the nutritional information that is so often confusing. Susie

Polmar and Kyle Robarge, for their help in research and updating of information.

My friend and boss Betsy Alexander, supervising producer at the *Today* show who along with all of our producers led by Jonathan Wald and Don Nash, help me to expand the knowledge and expertise of our viewers by encouraging me to produce the best reports that I can.

Bernie Swain, Harry Rhoads, Tony D'Amelio, and all the agents and staff at the Washington Speakers Bureau, for helping me get the consumers' voice heard in the boardrooms of American business.

Sterling Lord, my literary agent and one of the smartest and classiest men I know, who encouraged and inspired me to write this book.

A special thanks goes to my editor, Airié Dekidjiev, for her insights in breaking through the marketing message clutter, and for her vision in making *Being the Shopper* as influential as it can be.

Finally, I want to express my thanks to all the consumers who, over the past twenty-five years, have shared with me what they like and don't like about shopping, and to the millions more who know how important it is to voice their complaints as well as their compliments.

# ABOUT THE AUTHOR

The "Supermarket Guru®," Phil Lempert, is an expert in marketing analysis, issues, and trends for the food industry, and a respected analyst with an uncanny ability to identify and explain these trends to both industry and consumers. He is a highly regarded speaker, who travels the consumer products' world sharing his findings and insights into success.

Lempert was born into a food world started by his grandfather, also Philip, on a dairy farm in Belleville, New Jersey. His father, Sol, continued the family's food lines in snack-food manufacturing, importing, and distribution. Phil started his food career early, by checking the supermarket shelves with his dad, then working at McDonald's and Howard Johnson's in high school. After graduating Drexel University with a degree in marketing and retail management, he worked in his family's food brokerage firm. Never content to rely on passive merchandising, Lempert studied package design at Pratt Institute, and soon created an award-winning food-only advertising and marketing agency. In 1985, he began publishing *The Lempert Report*, and became the spokesman for food consumerism, which shifted his career to the editorial side of the food world.

A former columnist for both the *Chicago Tribune* and *Los Angeles Times*, Lempert is the food trends editor and on-air correspondent for NBC News' *Today* show, and featured on *Oprah*, *20/20*, *CNN*, *CNBC*, *MSNBC*, and Barbara Walters' *The View*, as well as on local television morning and news programs throughout the country. *Shopping Smart®* *with Phil Lempert* is a weekly live call-in radio show on the WOR Radio Network, and airs in over 100 cities nationwide. He also serves on the advisory board for the food marketing program at Western Michigan University.

SupermarketGuru.com was founded in 1995 and is a leading online resource, providing consumers with the latest information on trends, biotechnology, nutrition, food safety, new products, and shopping tips. More than 2.5 million visitors annually have access to breaking food-industry news, as well as participating in consumer panel surveys.

Mr. Lempert has been profiled and featured in such publications as the *New York Times, Wall Street Journal, Advertising Age, Brand Week,* and *Forbes.*

You can contact Phil at Plempert@SupermarketGuru.com.

# INDEX